LOURDES

Text written
in association with
Marie Caujolle

Translated by Alison Hebborn,
Géraldine Mattéra-Izett
and Barbara Jachowicz-Davoust

MSM

CONTENTS

Map of the Shrine

1

BERNADETTE

FROM LOURDES TO NEVERS

HER LIFE

HER VOCATION

HER PASSION

LOURDES – 12,500 YEARS OF HISTORY

At the foot of the Pyrenees, on the banks of the Gave de Pau, the town of Lourdes lies where the mountains come down to meet the plain. Overshadowed to the south by the first limestone foothills of the Pyrenees, Lourdes is bordered to the north by the Tarbes Plain and to the west by the Pau Plain.

This privileged site has always held an attraction for mankind, and the region was already inhabited 12,500 years ago. The Espélugues Caves constitute one of the most important Upper Paleolithic sites in the Pyrenees. Although the site was destroyed in the 19th century by disorganised digs, some remarkable finds were made there, including flint tools, reindeer antler sticks and spearheads. Often decorated with animal figures, they show clear evidence of the artistic talents of the early people of Lourdes. The most precious piece, a little horse carved from mammoth ivory, was discovered by Leon Nelli, son of Isidore Nelli, the contractor who built the Rosary Basilica.

As early as 56 B.C., the Romans, realising the strategic importance of the site, built the first fortress at the top of the limestone spur. From the 5th to the 7th centuries, the fortress was altered a number of times by the different peoples – Vandals, Alans, Visigoths, Vascons and Franks – who successively invaded Aquitaine. Later, the town was occupied by the Saracens as they retreated south after their defeat at the hands of Charles Martel at Poitiers in 732. In the 9th century, the lands of Bigorre were raised to the rank of county, and the counts of Bigorre took up residence in Lourdes castle. From there they could control fifty kilometres of their frontier, defend access to Bigorre and protect trade between the people of the mountains and the inhabitants of the plain.

In about 1195, the castle became the property of the viscount of Tartas, after which, no longer used as a feudal residence, it was passed from hand to hand as alliances were successively forged and broken off.

In 1216, at the height of his crusade against the Albigensians, Simon de Montfort, visiting the region to celebrate the marriage of his son, Guy, to Petronilla of Bigorre, tried to take the castle (then allied with the Cathars and defended by Nuño Sanche) but abandoned the attempt after a short siege.

In 1361, during the Hundred Years' War, Bigorre was ceded to the Prince of Wales, the famous Black Prince. He entrusted the command of the castle to Peter-Arnold and John of Béarn, who, with a gang of Gascon mercenaries, set about looting the area. In 1373, the duke of Anjou and Du Guesclin unsuccessfully

The Eagle and the Trout

In 778, the year of the Battle of Roncevalles, the Emperor Charlemagne besieged the fortress of Lourdes, occupied by the Saracens. As starvation threatened, an eagle fortuitously dropped a trout at the feet of Mirat, the Saracen commander.

A cunning fellow, Mirat had the fish sent to Charlemagne to give the impression that he still had plenty of food. Charlemagne was about to lift the siege when the Bishop of Le Puy, who was with him, had an inspired thought – Mirat should surrender, not to the emperor, but to the Queen of Heaven.

The idea appealed to the Saracen who laid down his arms at the feet of the Black Virgin of Le Puy and was baptised as Lorus. His name was given to the town, which in time became Lourdes. And since then, its coat of arms bears an eagle holding a silver trout in its beak.

besieged the castle. Four years later, in 1377, Gaston Fébus, count of Foix and Béarn, undertook to deliver the fortress into the hands of the king of France, but was unable to force it to surrender. The English were eventually driven out in 1407. In 1425, the castle became the property of the house of Foix, then, during the Wars of Religion, it fell into the hands of the Huguenot leader, Montgomery, loyal lieutenant of Joan of Albret, although he occupied it for little more than a fortnight. Only in 1607, when the county of Bigorre became part of France, did the castle become crown property. Henry IV of Navarre, King of France and heir to the counts of Foix, commissioned its restoration, entrusting the task to his governors. From then on, the walls of the old castle were to need little defending as few assaults, apart from an earthquake in 1660 which seriously damaged the chapel, were to assail them. During the French Revolution and the Napoleonic period, the proud citadel was used as a state prison.

In the early 1850's, shortly before the apparitions, Lourdes was a modest district town with a population of 4,135. The castle was occupied by an infantry garrison and the town itself was little more than a staging-post for travellers on their way to the spa towns of Barèges, Cauterets, Luz-Saint-Sauveur and Bagnères-de-Bigorre, and for pioneering mountaineers on their way to Gavarnie. A busy little town, Lourdes was the seat of the local magistrates court and home to a number of government offices. Its notables included civil servants, landed gentry, and members of the professional classes who published their own newspaper, *Le Lavedan*, and formed a free-thinkers' club that met in the Café Français. The middle classes consisted of craftsmen, shopkeepers, white-collar workers and wealthy farmers, while the working class was made up mainly of quarrymen and day-labourers who worked the towns' 164 farms. East of the town, on the banks of the Lapaca, five mills fought over the wheat harvest...

The Pyrenees Museum

The Pyrenees Museum, created by Louis Le Bondidier, for whom "nothing that is from the Pyrenees should be foreign to us", and by his wife, Margalide, in 1920, is located in the fortress-castle of Lourdes. And of course, "Pyreneism" has a special presentation room. The collections in the rooms showing the dairy industry, agriculture, furniture and costumes consist of many traditional costumes, furniture, tools and daily objects -- testimony of a period that has now disappeared. A Bearn-style kitchen and a Bigourdan-style bedroom, both of which date from the 19th century, have been reconstructed. Crockery made of porcelain and earthenware are presented in the room of domestic furnishings and weaving; harnesses used for horses and mules in the Harness Room (Sellerie); musical instruments from the 18th and 19th centuries in the Music Room; and "mourning candles" in the Wax Room. Excavations in the cave at Espéluges have provided important stone findings that are presented in the section on paleontology and archaeology. Part of the furnishings from the town's former parish church, destroyed in 1904, have been gathered together in the Castle's Notre Dame Chapel. And on the terrace, monuments and villages of the region, from both the north and the south of the Pyrenees, have been reconstituted on a 1/10 scale. As a bonus, from the top of its keep, the castle offers the visitor a superb view over the town and its shrines.

Flint spear point found by Nansouty

An Exceptional Environment

Lourdes is the key that provides access to the most spectacular sites in the Pyrenees, including the Cirque de Gavarnie. And even near the town itself, there is no shortage of natural beauty spots. Easily recognizable by its huge cross, which is lit up at night, the Pic du Jer rises to a height of 948 metres. A funicular railway leads to the top from which there is a wonderful view of the Tarbes and Pau plains and of the Pyrenees. A viewpoint indicator helps visitors pick out the main peaks in the chain. Three kilometres from town, amateur fishermen and water sports enthusiasts will be delighted by the Lac de Lourdes (Lourdes Lake) Formed by glaciation, this lake is one of the largest in the Pyrenees (55 hectares). On its southern shore, set among gentle valleys and pinewoods, there is an eighteen-hole golf course. There are many caves in the limestone foothills of the Pyrenees, but

The valley and the Cirque of Gavarnie

The caves of Bétharram and the Salle des Lustres

Bétharram caves will astonish even the most blasé! They are said to have been discovered by shepherds in 1819, but were not explored until 1899 Opened to the public early this century by Léon Ross, a painter, they were the first to make the wonders of the underground world known to tourists. Bétharram is also of scientific interest as the site provides an explanation of how caves of this kind are formed. An underground path, some three kilometres long, leads through five successive levels of galleries. Here, in the depths of the earth, stalactites and stalagmites have taken on strange shapes, such as giant bells, minarets, or human heads. And the river has worked the rock into huge sculptures and hollowed out vast chambers. South of Bagnères-de-Bigorre, a spa located

Bagnères-de-Bigorre:
a half-timbered house

The Pic du Midi de
Bigorre: Tourelle Dome

about twenty kilometres from Lourdes, the Pic du Midi de Bigorre overlooks the ski resort of La Mongie and the Tourmalet Pass from its height of 2,877 metres. Its altitude and its location have made it one of the best sites in the world for astronomical observations. During the early years of the 20th century, an observatory was built at its summit. Since June, 2000, a new cable car leaving from La Mongie carries passengers up. In fine weather, from the Pic's terraces, the visitor takes in the immense panorama of the Pyrenees range. In the museum centre, visitors can see models of telescopes currently in use and of Bernard Lyot's first coronagraph, an image of the sun taken by a coelostat and projected directly onto a screen, and can also be introduced to astronomy and earth sciences.

2

THE SOUBIROUS, FROM WATER MILL TO PRISON CELL

The Castérot family had worked Boly Mill since 1786 and fully intended buying it one day. But on July 1st, 1841, their plans were dramatically upset when Justin Castérot was killed in a cart accident, leaving a wife, four daughters and a little boy. His widow, Claire, unable to run the mill alone, decided she must find a man to take over the lease. Her choice fell upon François Soubirous, who worked in a neighbouring mill and who was still a bachelor at thirty-four. He was invited to court the eldest girl, Bernarde, the "heiress", as was the custom, but against all expectations, he fell in love with her younger sister Louise, a pretty sixteen year-old blonde. François was so determined that, having tried in vain to make him change his mind, Claire Castérot eventually relented. The wedding day was set for November 19th, 1842. However, only the civil ceremony took place that day, for François had just lost his mother; the church wedding was postponed until January 9th, 1843.

On January 7th, 1844, Louise gave birth to a little girl. Two days later, the child was baptised in the parish church of Saint Peter's (which was demolished in 1905). She was christened Marie-Bernarde, but would always be known as Bernadette.

But the young couple's happiness was soon to be overshadowed by misfortune: a tallow candle set fire to Louise's blouse and burnt her breast, leaving her unable to feed Bernadette. So for eighteen months the baby girl went to stay with a wet-nurse, Marie Laguës, who lived with her husband, Basile, in Burg House in the nearby village of Bartrès.

François Soubirous

Louise Soubirous

On April 1st, 1846, François brought his daughter home to the mill, where Louise was now expecting another child. On September 17th, she bore a second daughter, Toinette. The Soubirous and the Castérots were now living eight in three rooms. Such overcrowding placed so great a strain on relationships that, in 1848, the grandmother decided to take her other children and go to live with her eldest daughter who was now married.

On their own now, François and Louise set to work. But without Claire Castérot's experience, and too accommodating with their customers, they soon had money troubles. To add to their difficulties, the times were changing, and the new steam-powered mills were beginning to threaten their livelihood.

Other misfortunes fell upon them. In 1849, François was blinded in the left eye by a chip of stone while working on a millstone. And on January 4th, 1851, their young son Jean-Marie died. But then, on May 13th, Louise bore another son, naming him after his dead brother.

In 1852, their financial situation worsened. The mill was sold and the new owner decided to work it himself. The family still lived there, but François had to look for work elsewhere. Unable to pay the rent, on June 24th, 1854, the couple were forced to leave Boly Mill.

Now the Soubirous fell upon hard times. In 1855, a cholera epidemic claimed thirty-eight victims in Lourdes. Bernadette recovered, but her illness left her with chronic asthma. In the same year, Claire Castérot died, leaving François and Louise nine hundred francs with which they rented the mill at Arcizac-ez-Angles. But then, in 1856, the harvest failed through drought. For the Soubirous family it meant ruin and eviction. They ended up at Rives House, a miserable hovel, but their resources were so limited that they could not afford even that modest rent. Penniless and homeless, at the beginning of 1857, they moved into the *cachot* – the punishment cell of the disused prison – a filthy hole that a cousin lent them out of kindness. In order to survive, the

Boly Mill: The interior

Door of the "cachot"

whole family had to work. François became a day-labourer; Louise a cleaning-woman. Bernadette looked after her brothers and sister, collected bones and scrap iron which she sold to the rag-and-bone woman, and even helped out in her aunt's tavern. But these meagre sources of income were no more than stopgaps, and barely enough to make ends meet. Times were hard indeed, and famine raged throughout the whole region. The crisis was so serious that the Emperor Napoleon III even had sacks of flour distributed.

On March 27th, 1857, tragedy struck the Soubirous family again: the baker Maisongrosse accused François of stealing. Arrested and imprisoned, he was released a week later through lack of evidence, and returned, a broken man, to the *cachot*. Reduced first from master-miller to day-labourer, public disgrace was now added to loss of social status, leaving him little more than a pauper suspected of theft.

In September 1857, so as to make "one less mouth to feed", Bernadette went into service as a farm-girl with her old wet-nurse at Bartrès, and so returned to Burg House. Now thirteen years old, Bernadette still could not read or write as, once again, she was forced to leave school. Nevertheless, she had been promised that she would be allowed to prepare for her first Communion.

On the farm, Bernadette felt very homesick. During the day, she minded the sheep and did the household chores and, in the evening, Marie Laguës tried to teach her the catechism. But Bernadette, who spoke only the local dialect, simply could not remember the answers she had to make in French and, as often as not, these lessons ended in shouting and tears.

In January 1858, she managed to persuade her parents to let her return to Lourdes. As an excuse to the Laguës family, she told a white lie saying, "*Monsieur le Curé* wants me to prepare for my first Communion".

Returning to the *cachot* on January 21st, she began attending the paupers' class at the hospice run by the Sisters of Charity of Nevers.

Bartrès: Burg House

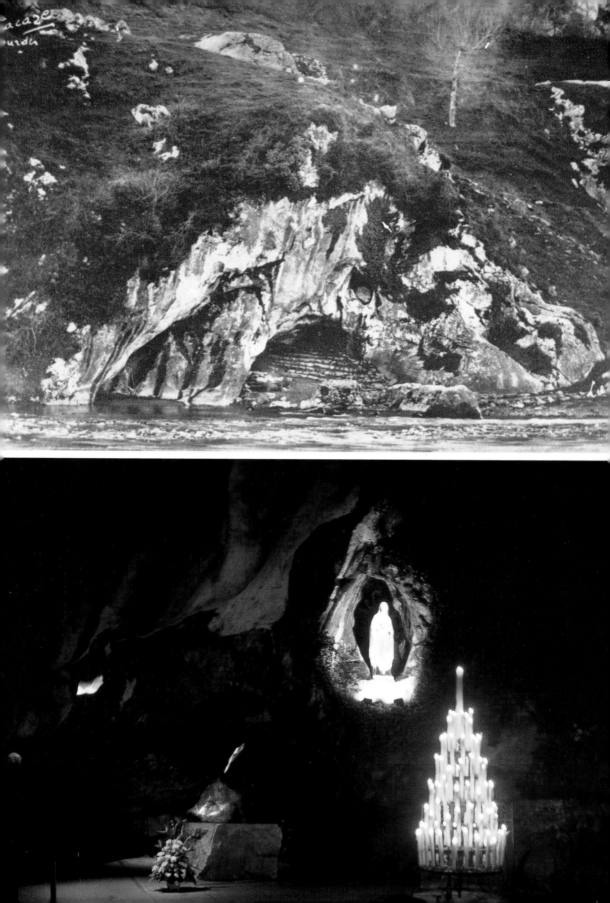

3

THE EIGHTEEN APPARITIONS

On Thursday, February 11th, 1858, the fire in the hearth of the *cachot* went out, because the lost log had been sold the previous day to buy food. Bernadette, who was now fourteen, set off for the woods with her sister Toinette and a friend, Jeanne Abadie, nicknamed Baloume. The girls walked over the Pont Vieux and past Savy Mill, and then followed the millstream which flowed into the Gave near a natural grotto in Massabielle Rock. Inside the grotto they spotted a pile of dead wood. What a godsend! Toinette and Baloume took off their clogs and, with no more ado, crossed the stream. Bernadette, not wanting to get her feet wet, asked the others to help, but they refused. As she began taking her clogs off, a rushing sound like "a gust of wind" made her look up. Looking towards the grotto, she saw "a Lady in white". Frightened, she seized her rosary. The Apparition made the sign of the cross. Bernadette did the same and began to pray. When the vision was over, she hurried to catch up with Toinette and Baloume.

"Didn't you see anything just then?" she asked. "No. Did you?" came the reply.

"Well, if you didn't, then I didn't either." Intrigued, her sister pressed her further, and Bernadette, having made her promise not to tell anyone, described what had happened. But when they got home, Toinette was unable to hold her tongue and told their mother! Fearing some new misfortune, Louise grew angry and told her elder daughter that she was never to return to the grotto. Two days later, Bernadette was still worried about the apparition and told her confessor, Father Pomian, what had happened. With her permission, he in turn told the parish priest, Father Peyramale, who thought it of no great importance.

On Sunday, February 14th, with her father's permission, Bernadette returned to Massa-

Bernadette's Account of the First Apparition*

"I went to the banks of the Gave to gather wood with two other little girls. They crossed the water and started to cry. When I asked them why they were crying, they said that the water was cold. I asked them to help me throw stones in the water so that I could cross without taking my clogs off; they said I would have to do as they had done. So I went a little way further on to see if I could find a place to cross without getting my feet wet. I could not. So I came back in front of the grotto. Just as I started to take my clogs off, I heard a rustling sound. I looked towards the meadow; I could see that the trees were not moving at all. I turned back to my clogs. Again I heard the rustling sound. This time I raised my head and looked towards the grotto. I saw a Lady dressed in white; she had a white robe with a blue belt and a yellow rose on each foot, the same colour as the chain of her rosary. When I saw her, I rubbed my eyes; I thought I must be mistaken. I put my hand in my pocket to find my rosary. I wanted to make the sign of the cross but I could not lift my hand to my forehead: it fell back down. The Vision made the sign of the cross. Then my hand trembled; I tried again to make the sign and this time managed to. I went through my rosary; the Vision ran her own beads through her fingers, but did not move her lips. When I had finished my rosary, the Vision suddenly disappeared. I asked the other two girls if they had seen anything; they said they had not."

_____
* Written on May 28th, 1861

bielle. With her were some other girls who had brought along a flask of holy water. The Lady was still there. She smiled at Bernadette as she had the first time. Sprinkling her with holy water, the girl pleaded, "If you are from God, then stay; if not, go away". As the Lady continued to smile, Bernadette began to pray. So intense was her ecstasy that her friends took fright and ran for help to Savy Mill. When Louise heard of it, she came running, stick in hand, to put an end to these trips to the grotto.

The news was soon the talk of the town. Madame Milhet, a wealthy lady for whom Louise did odd jobs, was intrigued. Thinking back to the little girl in the congregation of the Children of Mary who had died the previous October, she wondered, "Supposing it were Elisa Latapie's ghost." With her seamstress, the bailiff's daughter, Antoinette Peyret, she decided to accompany Bernadette to the grotto. They set out early in the morning of Thursday, February 18th. Bernadette, who had been told to ask the Lady to write her name, held out the pen and writing case brought along by Antoinette Peyret. At this request, the vision spoke for the first time, in patois, saying, "That is not necessary… Will you be so kind as to come here every day for a fortnight?… I promise you happiness, not in this world, but in the next".

Back in Lourdes, the rumour soon spread that Bernadette could see the Holy Virgin. People's curiosity was aroused. On February 19th, eight people were present for the fourth apparition. The next day there were thirty. On Sunday, February 21st, more than a hundred watched as the Lady appeared to Bernadette for the sixth time. Concerned for public order, Police Superintendent Jacomet submitted Bernadette to an official interrogation that very evening. "So, Bernadette, you see the Holy Virgin, do you?"

"I never said I saw the Holy Virgin."

"Oh, so you didn't see anything, then?"

"Well, yes I did. I saw a little lady."

And, cautiously, systematically using the patois word *Aquerò* (meaning *that*) to refer to the

Superintendent Jacomet

Police Superintendent Jacomet had been stationed in Lourdes since November 1853. An educated, intelligent and popular man, he had displayed great courage and devotion to duty during the cholera epidemic in the winter of 1855. He knew the Soubirous family, and especially François, whom he had arrested on suspicion of theft. Dominique Jacomet was highly skilled in the art of interrogation. Able to detect the smallest signs of guilt, he was particularly good at getting suspects to make admissions. He knew how to alternate between friendliness and threats, and how to switch from being ingratiating one moment to intimidating the next. Such talent, however, was of little use when, on Sunday, February 21st, 1858, Jacomet took down Bernadette's first statement. Faced with the girl's simplicity and obvious sincerity, he was forced to admit defeat.

Police Superintendent Jacomet

Lady, Bernadette went on to tell her tale. Jacomet did not believe her and, trying to get at the truth through subterfuge, altered her statement. Unruffled, Bernadette spotted his mistakes, disputed them, and stuck to her original story. At last, running out of arguments, Jacomet asked François, who had come to fetch his daughter, to stop her going to the grotto. But Bernadette was adamant, saying, "But, sir, I promised to go back."

On Tuesday, February 23rd, she returned to Massabielle. The Lady was there, and so were a hundred and fifty curious onlookers. For the eighth apparition, on Wednesday, February 24th, three hundred people watched as Bernadette made her way forward on her knees, then kissed the ground. When questioned, she explained, "The Lady said to me, 'Penitence, penitence, penitence' and then 'Pray God for the conversion of sinners… Go and kiss the ground in penitence for sinners'."

On Thursday, February 25th, the day of the ninth apparition, after repeating the gestures of penitence made the previous day, Bernadette suddenly got up and made her way hesitantly towards the Gave, where she stopped abruptly, turned around and went to kneel on the left of the grotto. There she dug a hole which began to fill with muddy water. Three times she tried to drink from it, but spat it out in disgust. Only at the fourth attempt did she manage to swallow some. Then she washed her face with the water and fed a handful of grass to her mouth. At the sight of Bernadette covered in mud and chewing grass, the three hundred and fifty onlookers were scandalised and cried out in indignation. But Bernadette remained unmoved. She was only doing what *Aquerò* had told her, saying, "Go and drink from the spring and wash yourself in it".

That evening Bernadette was summoned before the Imperial Prosecutor, Dutour. Refusing to be intimidated, she stuck firmly to her tale. She had promised to return to the grotto, and so she did, on the 27th and 28th of February, for the tenth and eleventh apparitions.

Imperial Prosecutor Dutour

Imperial Prosecutor Dutour was, like Jacomet, worried about the threat to public order posed by Bernadette's visions. Was it trickery, or was the girl mad? At all events, she had to be prevented from going back to Massabielle. It would be easy to persuade her father, whom he had already dealt with over a matter of suspected theft, to keep the girl at home. But François Soubirous was away and Dutour was received by the mother and daughter. In a distant manner, to hide his scorn, he questioned Bernadette closely, affably at first, before becoming more intimidating. But the girl remained calm, explaining her "scandalous" conduct quite simply: it was for sinners. Even the threat of prison had no effect; she had promised to return to the grotto. The report made, on March 1st, by an exasperated Dutour was disparaging of the whole family.

Imperial Prosecutor Dutour

At Massabielle, clear water now flowed from the hole Bernadette had dug. On March 1st, the day of the twelfth apparition, Catherine Latapie recovered the use of her paralysed hand after bathing it in water from the spring. On March 2nd, after the thirteenth apparition, Bernadette went with her two aunts to see *Monsieur le Curé*, the parish priest, Father Peyramale. She brought him a message. The Lady had said to her, "Let the people come in procession and let a chapel be built here". But Father Peyramale did not believe in these apparitions and she barely had time to give the first part of her message before she was called a liar and told to leave. But the girl persisted and returned to the presbytery that same evening. Father Peyramale and his curates listened to her in amazement. Then, still incredulous, he told her to ask the Lady her name. The next day, three thousand people crowded round the grotto, causing the authorities considerable alarm. That evening, Bernadette tackled the priest again; "The Lady still wants her chapel". Exasperated, he repeated his request; "Get her to say her name", then added, "and make the rosebush at the grotto blossom". At dawn on Thursday, March 4th, 1858, for the "big day", the last of the fifteen, eight thousand people waited at the grotto, hoping for some sign, although there was to be none. Bernadette repeated all the actions previously requested by the Apparition: she went forward on her knees to the spring, drank from it, washed in it, and kissed the ground for sinners. Her ecstasy had lasted three quarters of an hour and still the Lady had not said her name. The crowd began to disperse, disappointed but calm. Later, a number of people gathered outside the *cachot* to see Bernadette, have her touch their rosaries, and even offer her money, which she refused, saying, "It burns me". With the fortnight of the visions over, Bernadette went back to school. But the grotto at Massabielle was constantly full of visitors, and lit day and night by increasing numbers of candles brought by the faithful.

"Monsieur le Curé"

"He combined an apostle's heart with an unusually resolute kind of common sense and a character that nothing could budge when it came to the truth," wrote Henri Lasserre of Father Peyramale, known to Bernadette as *Monsieur le Curé*. From a middle-class background, "the priest of the apparitions in Lourdes" had first been curate, then chaplain of the military hospital in Tarbes. He had been given the parish of Lourdes in 1851, and he ran it energetically and with a firm hand, his strong personality earning him the fear and respect of his parishioners. Father Peyramale became one of Bernadette's most ardent defenders, fiercely resisting an attempt to have her committed to a mental hospital in March 1858, and protecting her from curious sightseers by finding her a place, in August of that year, in the local hospice run by the Sisters of Charity of Nevers.

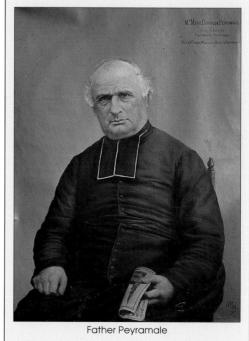

Father Peyramale

On March 25th, during the night, Bernadette felt she was being "called" again. At five in the morning she went to the grotto. Three times she asked the Lady her name: "Please, *Mademoiselle*, would you be so kind as to tell me who you are?" But all she received in reply was a smile. She tried again; this time *Aquerò* clasped her hands together and, lifting her eyes heavenwards, said in patois, "*Que soy era Immaculada Councepciou*" (I am the Immaculate Conception). After this sixteenth apparition, Bernadette went directly to see Father Peyramale: "*Aquerò* said, 'I am the Immaculate Conception'!" "But what are you saying? Do you know what that means?" asked the priest. "No, but I kept saying the name to myself all the way here," replied Bernadette. Shaken by this revelation, Father Peyramale sent her home. How could this child know the dogma proclaimed four years earlier by Pope Pius IX? He decided to inform Monsignor Laurence, bishop of Tarbes, straight away. Only that evening did Bernadette learn the meaning of the Lady's words.

For twelve days, nothing happened. Then, on Wednesday, April 7th, Bernadette went to the grotto for what was to be the seventeenth apparition. Caught up in her ecstasy, she did not notice as the flame of her candle licked at her fingers for nearly ten minutes. Doctor Dozous, a notorious sceptic, was present. Examining the girl's hands afterwards, he could find no trace of a burn. He would be one of the first to be converted in Lourdes.

From then on, Bernadette concentrated on her schoolwork and on preparing her first Communion, which she took on June 3rd, 1858. At Massabielle, Louis Bouriette, Blaisette Cazenave and Henri Busquet were suddenly healed by contact with water from the spring. Following certain displays of excess zeal, the authorities forbade access to the grotto and boarded it up. On July 16th, Bernadette went in secret to the bank of the Gave opposite the grotto, and met her Lady for the eighteenth, and last, time. "I never saw her look so lovely," she said.

The Dogma of the Immaculate Conception

The dogma of the Immaculate Conception affirms that the Virgin Mary was "preserved immaculate from all stain of original sin" from "the first instant of her conception". The recognition of so singular a grace was to kindle controversy and spark passionate debate for nearly nine centuries as theologians struggled to reconcile this idea with the principle of universal redemption. The problem was this: how could Jesus be the Saviour of a human creature who had been exempt from sin from the moment of conception? Saint Augustine in the 5th century and Saint Bernard in the 12th were the first to point out this apparent contradiction which was to be resolved in the 12th century by the theologian Duns Scotus who argued that the Virgin Mary enjoyed "anticipated redemption". The matter, however, was still not settled when, on November 27th, 1830, the Virgin Mary gave a sign to the Church: a young novice by the name of Catherine Labouré had a vision in which she was told to have a medallion struck bearing the words: "O Mary, conceived without sin, pray for us who turn to you". So it was the Virgin Mary herself who defined herself as "conceived without sin", and who asked to be addressed in those terms when called upon in prayer. The issue continued to be the subject of much discussion until 1854 when, on December 8th, Pope Pius IX, with the support of bishops all over the world, promulgated the dogma making the "Immaculate Conception" of Mary an article of faith in his encyclical *Ineffabilis Deus*. And then, by a remarkable coincidence, on March 25th, 1858, the Virgin Mary herself appeared to Bernadette as the "Immaculate Conception".

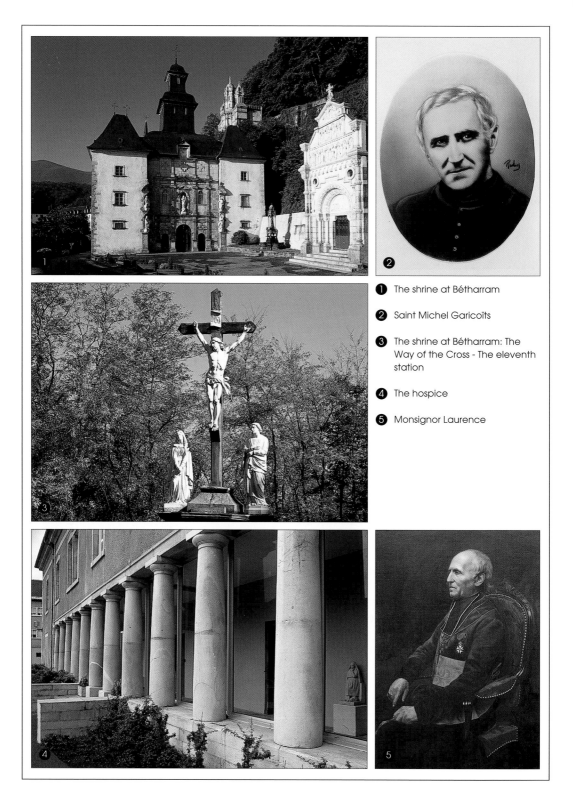

1. The shrine at Bétharram

2. Saint Michel Garicoïts

3. The shrine at Bétharram: The Way of the Cross - The eleventh station

4. The hospice

5. Monsignor Laurence

THE BIRTH OF A VOCATION

On July 28th, 1858, the bishop of Tarbes ordered a commission of inquiry into the events that had taken place in Lourdes. Bernadette, who had already been questioned six times by the civil authorities, was now, and over the next four years, to be confronted by the ecclesiastical powers. Throughout, she faced her interrogators calmly, confidently and modestly, never changing or embellishing her story. On October 5th, the Emperor Napoleon III had the grotto opened again. Soon, police reports began recording the presence of more than a hundred people at the grotto every day. Spontaneous religious ceremonies took place. On July 5th, 1859, the word "pilgrimage" was used for the first time in an official report. At the same time, new unexplained healings were occurring. Justin Bouhort, Madeleine Rizan and Marie Moreau were each restored to health by the waters of Massabielle. The fame of the town was such that, in August 1859, the Emperor himself came to visit.

Bernadette continued to attend the classes run by the Sisters of Charity of Nevers, but her daily life had become extremely difficult as crowds of visitors thronged incessantly round the Soubirous' door. To protect her from the curious gaze of these sightseers, in July 1860, Father Peyramale found a place for her in the boarding-house at the Sisters' hospice. Here Bernadette made rapid progress in reading and writing. In 1861 she wrote her first account of the Apparitions (see page 19).

At last, on January 18th, 1862, after four years of extensive investigations, based on reconstructions, eyewitness accounts, and Bernadette's own statements, Monsignor Laurence published the verdict of his inquiry: "We consider that the Immaculate Mary, Mother of God, really did appear to Bernadette Soubirous on February 11th, 1858 and the following

The Saint of Bétharram

Father Garicoïts would sometimes come to Boly Mill to beg a few sacks of flour for the poor. Born on April 15th, 1797, at Ibarre in the Basque Country, Michel Garicoïts founded the community of the Priests of the Sacred Heart of Jesus. These "crack troops", as he called them, lived by a strict rule of devotion, absolute obedience, gentleness and simplicity. It was at the seminary in Bétharram, where he was Father Abbot, that the first community was established. In addition to this order of priests, and at the insistence of the lay congregation, Father Garicoïts also founded a community of friars. He had the shrine of Our Lady of Bétharram and the Calvary restored, and opened a school and a college on the site. The shrine of Our Lady of Bétharram owes its origin to a statue of the Virgin Mary said to have been found by shepherds in the 14th century in a burning bush beside the Gave. A chapel was built on the spot. A little while later, according to legend, a girl was saved from drowning by the Virgin Mary, who held out a branch to her. "O, lou beth arram!" (Oh, the lovely branch!), the girl is said to have cried. Her words were soon adopted as the name of the shrine, and a pilgrimage, which takes place each year on September 14th, was organised. On July 30th, 1858, at the request of the bishop of Tarbes, Bernadette met the man already known as the "Saint of Bétharram". Michel Garicoïts seems to have had a profound influence on her and, in particular, her choice of vocation. He died in 1863 and was canonised in 1947.

days, a total of eighteen times, in the grotto at Massabielle near the town of Lourdes, that the Apparition possesses all the characteristics of truth, and that the faithful are justified in believing it to be genuine. We authorise within our diocese the worship of Our Lady of the Grotto of Lourdes."

His statement also gave official recognition to the first seven miraculous cures.

At Massabielle, building work began. The town council ceded Espélugues Hill and the riverbank near the Grotto to the bishopric. And roads were renamed, with Rue de la Carrerète and Rue du Baous becoming Rue de la Grotte. However, Bernadette's health was failing. In March 1862, she fell ill with pneumonia. Her condition became so serious that on April 28th she received the Extreme Unction. Her spectacular recovery puzzled the doctors, and the town was full of talk of a new miracle, although it was, in fact, no more than one of the sudden remissions that often occur with asthma. From 1862 to 1866, her illness forced her to spend considerable stretches of time in the mountains, especially in Cauterets. In May 1862, four girls came to say good-bye to her before they left for their novitiate in Nevers Convent. Bernadette told them, "I know I am to become a nun; but I don't know yet to which order I am to belong. The Holy Virgin hasn't told me; I'm waiting".

On October 14th, 1862, sixty labourers, including François Soubirous, began building work on the Crypt. Busy with her schoolwork, Bernadette was unaware that the construction work had begun. "Now I'm just like everyone else", she declared, showing what a happy and well-adjusted teenager she was. Now that the visions were over, Bernadette spent her time between school and caring for the sick.

In the autumn of 1863, the rich Latour sisters commissioned a statue of Our Lady of Lourdes from Joseph Fabisch, a sculptor from Lyons. Made of marble, this statue of the Virgin Mary was to replace the small stucco one that had been placed temporarily in the Grotto. Fabisch

Bernadette, Just an Ordinary Girl

Far from being trapped in the role of a plaster saint, Bernadette was an ordinary girl – lively, cheerful, and perhaps even a little vain. One day she was found letting out her skirt to make it more like a crinoline – that voluminous petticoat which the clergy, at the time, qualified as "diabolical". On another occasion, she was discovered putting a piece of wood inside the bodice of her dress to increase the size of her bust. "Bernadette is the real life and soul of the playground," reported the Sisters. "Always happy and gay, she leads the little children in their dancing games, even though she is soon out of breath." And Bernadette, who enjoyed the company of children and liked playing with them, was soon asked to look after the younger ones. In the schoolroom, she would make her classmates laugh. "You'd have to stuff the book into my head!" she exclaimed one day, when she could not remember her lesson. Avoiding all serious topics, especially that of the apparitions, her relations with her friends were natural, despite her fame. But Bernadette had her faults, too, mainly that of obstinacy; she knew what she wanted. One day she stood up to a Sister who wanted her, albeit for no good reason, to change her Sunday dress. And when she was not allowed home to visit her family, she protested, exclaiming, "They promised!" Fond of her food, she got round a ban on trips to the vegetable garden by throwing her clog from a window so that a friend could fill it with strawberries for her. This incident was examined at great length during Bernadette's canonisation procedure. The devil's advocate laid particular stress on this trick, which he saw as a serious breach of discipline. Today, such naughtiness just makes us smile.

The statue of the Apparition in the Grotto ▶

QUE SOY
ERA
IMMACULADA COUNCEPCION!

MAISON PATERNELLE DE Ste BERNADETTE

was a specialist; he had already produced the statues of Our Lady on the spires of the basilicas at Fourvière (in Lyons) and La Salette (near Grenoble). On September 17th, he arrived in Lourdes to question Bernadette on the Virgin Mary's appearance. Spontaneously, Bernadette stood up and mimed what she had seen, clasping her hands together and raising her eyes heavenwards. Four months later, she was disappointed by Fabisch's overly academic representation of the Virgin Mary, and criticised it, saying, "She lifted her eyes, not her whole head. It looks as if she has a goitre!" On April 4th, 1864, before a crowd of twenty thousand, Monsignor Laurence blessed the statue. Engraved on its base are the words, in patois, that Our Lady spoke to Bernadette on Thursday, March 25th, during the sixteenth apparition: *Que soy era Immaculada Councepciou* (I am the Immaculate Conception). The same day, Bernadette, who was too ill to attend the ceremony, decided to join the Sisters of Charity of Nevers. Her admission to the community, however, was not confirmed until November 1864, for the Mother General of Saint Gildard's Convent in Nevers had hesitated before taking on such a famous novice.

In February 1865, Bernadette began her postulancy at the hospice in Lourdes. All the while continuing her instruction, sometimes she helped the nursing sister care for the sick, and sometimes she looked after the younger pupils. In April 1866, she made her formal request to become a novice to Mother Vauzou, mistress of novices in Nevers, and was accepted. On May 19th, 1866, Monsignor Laurence blessed the Crypt, and two days later, forty thousand pilgrims attended Solemn Mass. Bernadette followed the proceedings incognito, dressed in the uniform of the Children of Mary. On July 3rd, she went to the Grotto one last time to pray, then spent the evening with her family in Lacadé Mill, where the Soubirous had been living since 1865.

The following day, Wednesday, July 4th, 1866, she left her home town, never to return.

Bernadette and the Children of Mary

5

SISTER MARIE-BERNARD

On July 7th, 1866, Bernadette arrived at Saint Gildard's Convent in Nevers. The next day, she was ushered into the novitiate hall to tell the tale of the apparitions once and for all before the assembled community. Her story told, Bernadette entered into silence and began her training. "I've come here to hide," she pointed out on her arrival. The mistress of novices, Mother Marie-Thérèse Vauzou wondered how she should treat this girl known as "Mary's favoured one", whose presence attracted so many people to the convent. Deciding to be twice as hard on Bernadette as on any other new Sister, she spent much of her time making sure that all displays of pride in the girl were thoroughly quashed. "The girl's useless!" was the cry that would accompany Bernadette throughout her novitiate.

On July 29th, Bernadette donned her nun's habit as Sister Marie-Bernard. A fortnight later she fell ill and was taken to the infirmary. Her condition deteriorated rapidly until, on October 25th, she was at death's door. The bishop of Nevers, Monsignor Forcade, administered the Extreme Unction and, as a precautionary measure, had Bernadette take her vows in advance. The next day, she seemed much better and, unprompted, declared that she knew she was out of danger. Although severely censured, she was allowed to keep the veil. On December 8th, 1866, during her convalescence, she learnt of her mother's death.

On February 2nd, fully recovered, she returned to the novitiate where Mother Marie-Thérèse Vauzou greeted her with the words, "Now begins the time of trial".

Sister Marie-Bernard

Louise Soubirous

Sister Marie-Bernard returned to her training. She never complained of the somewhat excessive severity of the mistress of novices. "Mother Mistress is right," she would say, "because I am very proud… I shall work at trying to improve myself."

On October 30th, 1867, before the whole community, Bernadette renewed her vows: poverty, chastity, obedience and charity. That evening, the newly professed nuns were placed under obedience by the bishop and the Mother General, that is, they were allotted the specific tasks they were to undertake within the community. Bernadette learnt that she was to remain in the mother house. The bishop had assigned her a position "nowhere", and given her the task of prayer. In practice, she became assistant to the convent's nurse, Sister Marthe Forest. On April 12th, 1870, Sister Marthe fell seriously ill, remaining bedridden until her death. Bernadette took over her duties. How ironic that this chronic invalid should, for three years, assume the role of head nurse!

For the first time in her life, Bernadette had real responsibility, and she applied herself to her task conscientiously and with remarkable skill. Concerned not only with providing medical care, she liked to reassure her patients, listen to them and counsel them. Wholeheartedly dedicated to her work, she even took on the rigours of night duty herself. The doctor of the mother house was full of praise for her work: "She looks after her patients very sensibly, and diligently follows all the treatment prescribed; consequently, she commands great authority and is, in my opinion, entirely trustworthy". These words were written in 1872 to refute the vicious attack made by Doctor Voisin of the Salpêtrière Hospital in Paris who had declared, "The miracle of Lourdes is based on no more than the statements of a demented child who is now shut away in the Ursuline Convent in Nevers". On July 19th, 1870, France declared war on Prussia. In August, the Mother Superior put her convent and her Sisters at the disposal of

"God is Everywhere, Even Among the Prussians"

On October 3rd, 1870, following a decision by the Ministry of War, Saint Gildard's Convent in Nevers was converted into a military hospital. Bernadette, who was then acting head nurse, cared for the wounded and assisted the chief doctor in the numerous operations he had to perform. As the enemy troops advanced towards Nevers, the military authorities consolidated the town's defences. By the end of November, artillery guns had been installed in the convent; the arrival of the Prussians was said to be imminent. The general panic that ensued seems to have spared Bernadette who remained calm and continued to perform her duties with her usual composure. "The only thing I'm afraid of is bad Catholics," she declared when questioned by one of the other nuns about the threat of invasion. On December 15th, the bishop of Nevers advised the Sisters to take a few precautionary safety measures and to leave the convent only as a last resort. On the 21st, the French general, Bourbaki, arrived with his army in Nevers. The nuns fled, leaving behind just a small group of assistant nurses under Bernadette's supervision. Soon the hospital was filled with both French and Prussian wounded. The Mother Superior recorded the numbers of sick and dead in her diary. Bernadette nursed them all, irrespective of nationality, perhaps even paying particular attention to the wounded Prussians. In a detailed letter to her father, she justified her actions saying, "God is everywhere, even among the Prussians. I remember, when I was little, after a sermon by *Monsieur le Curé*, I heard people saying, 'Well, he's only doing his job, isn't he?'. I think the Prussians are only doing their job, too."

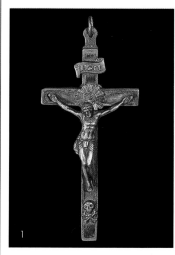

Nevers: Saint Gildard's Convent

1 The crucifix of Bernadette's profession of faith

2 Notre-Dame-des-Eaux

3 A holy water stoup in the chapel

4 Prayer books that once belonged to Bernadette

5 The inner corridor

the Ministry of War. During the period that followed, Bernadette wrote long letters to her father, in which she described daily life in the infirmary now that it had been turned into a military hospital. This beloved father died on March 4th, 1871. Greatly affected by his death, Bernadette threw herself into her work until, two years later, her health began to decline again. Having suffered a relapse in January 1873, she was to remain confined to her room as her convalescence was punctuated by new attacks. On June 3rd, 1873, she received the Extreme Unction for the third time.

On October 30th, she was officially relieved of her duties. Once fully recovered from her illness, Bernadette returned to her original post as assistant nurse, under the orders of the new head nurse, Sister Gabriel de Vigouroux. Having held a position of responsibility for so long, Bernadette found it difficult to adjust to her new situation. For a while she also took on the role of sacristy assistant, helping the choirboys dress and washing the sacred linen.

François Soubirous

In April 1875, she took to her bed once more. From then on, she was to remain a permanent invalid.

On September 8th, 1877, Father Peyramale died. On learning of his death, Bernadette announced to those around her, "It will soon be my turn now". But she would have to wait two years before her prediction came true; two years in which she endured a true martyrdom. She suffered piercing chest pains and vomited blood because of her chronic asthma. She was afflicted with aneurysm and gastralgia. A tumour on her knee meant that she had to use crutches. And finally a bone disease left her so disabled that she became bedridden.

By the spring of 1879, her whole body was little more than an open wound. On March 28th, her condition worsened further and, despite her refusal, the Extreme Unction was administered to her for a fourth time. Bernadette performed her act of contrition and asked forgiveness of the Mother Superior. Once again, she continued to live after these final sacraments, but spent Holy Week (from April 6th to 13th) in a state of extreme agony. During this period, she asked that all the pious images pinned to the drapes around her bed, which she called her "white chapel", be removed. She kept only her crucifix, which she had tied to her wrist. On Easter Monday, April 14th, this miller's daughter confided in Sister Léontine, "I'm ground down like a grain of wheat", and added, "I'd never have thought it took so much suffering to die". On the following Wednesday, April 16th, 1879, Sister Marie-Bernard asked to be lifted from her bed. She was helped into an armchair. At one o'clock that afternoon, the chaplain was summoned urgently to the patient's side. Bernadette made her confession, then recited the prayer for the dying, her eyes fixed all the while on her crucifix. Twice she intoned, "Holy Mary, Mother of God, pray for me, a poor sinner…".

Then Bernadette asked for a drink. Having made the sign of the cross, she swallowed a few sips of water, bowed her head, and died.

6

SAINT BERNADETTE

In 1909, as part of the procedure to canonise Bernadette, Pope Pius X instituted an inquiry into her "reputation of holiness". During the course of the inquiry, on September 9th, 1909, Bernadette's body was exhumed in the presence of the bishop of Nevers, the Mother Superior of the convent, the civil authorities and two forensic medical experts, Doctors Jourdan and David. All agreed on the facts of the matter; the nun's body appeared to be intact.

The forensic report of the first exhumation concentrated on describing the outward appearance of the corpse. Bernadette's skin, nails, teeth and hair seemed to be in perfect condition. Stranger still, her veins, which could be seen quite clearly through her skin, showed that her internal organs had also been spared the normal process of decay. In 1913, Rome once again took up the procedure to beatify and canonise Bernadette. During the First World War, however, the inquiry was suspended and it was not until the spring of 1919 that the second exhumation took place. The conclusions arrived at by the two new pathologists chosen to perform the autopsy, Doctors Comte and Talon, were similar to those of their predecessors.

In 1923, Pope Pius XI proclaimed the "heroic nature of the virtues" of Bernadette and ordered a final examination of her body before declaring her Blessed. On April 18th, 1925, forty-six years after her death, Bernadette's body was exhumed once more. This time the autopsy revealed the perfect condition of her internal organs. The surgeon, Dr. Comte, noted, in particular, the astonishingly well-preserved state of her liver, which is the organ of the human body most subject to decay.

Canonised in 1933 by Pope Pius XI, today, Bernadette lies in a glass casket in the chapel of Saint Gildard's Convent in Nevers.

The Autopsy Report of April 18th, 1925

"... As in 1919, there was no smell of putrefaction when the coffin was opened; none of the numerous people present seemed in any way put out or adversely affected... Apart from the fact that the ligaments are blacker than they were in 1919, it could be said that the body is just as well preserved now as it was six years ago; that is, it seems to have undergone a transformation process known as mummification. The parchment-like skin covers almost all the cadaver... Deep palpation reveals that the muscle tissue has retained a certain elasticity. In conclusion, I consider that we are dealing with a *mummified* corpse in a relatively good state of preservation."

The autopsy report of April 18th, 1925

2

PILGRIMS AND PILGRIMAGES

THE CAPITAL OF PRAYER

LIVING THE MESSAGE OF LOURDES

BERNADETTE
+
LOVRDES
+1858+

1

LOURDES TODAY

The Keys to the Message

The message from the Virgin Mary to Bernadette was simple. Poverty, prayer and penance were the keys that would open the kingdom of God. To teach Man the Lord's will, Mary, the servant of the Lord, had chosen the little shepherdess, a tavern servant who lived in a cell (Le Cachot) and gathered wood in the pigs' shelter. The Mother of Jesus – He who was born on the straw in Bethlehem – thus shows us that veritable wealth is that of the heart. First of all, Bernadette accepted the destitution her family suffered from because "God allowed it". Then, after the apparitions, she chose the side of the poor. In our materialistic world, Bernadette's commitment reminds believers of the importance of the simple life, altruism, charity and the meaning of sharing. Bernadette, "who knew her rosary" only in French, a language she didn't understand, experienced real prayer, beyond words, silent and joyous. In Lourdes, prayer is a dialogue with a God of love. "Virgin of Light, you are the smile of a God who loves us."

"Pray for the conversion of sinners", "Penance, penance, penance…" the Virgin told Bernadette, to whom she appeared "sad because of sinners" and asked her to "go and eat of that grass" for the sinners… Hence, she who was conceived without sin invites us to reflect upon sin and Evil. She calls for lucidity and the real penance that is sincere conversion.

The Adoration Tent

The Shrine

Centered on Massabielle Grotto, the shrine of Lourdes grew up little by little. In 1861, the town council ceded the rock and the adjacent riverbank to the bishopric of Tarbes. From 1861 to 1864, in order to improve access, the bishop, Monsignor Laurence, gradually bought up the surrounding land. In 1869, Espélugues Hill, on which the Way of the Cross is laid out, was added. And finally, between 1874 and 1942, the meadows on the right bank of the Gave near Massabielle were acquired. Today, this whole area is known as the domain of the Grotto and the Shrine of Our Lady of Lourdes. Covering a total surface area of fifty hectares, it is one of the biggest shrines in the world. Under the authority of the bishop of Tarbes and Lourdes, the shrine is directed by a rector and staffed by a number of chaplains. Access to the shrine is gained through any of seven gates situated at each of the four points of the compass: to the south, Saint Joseph's Gate, the Lacets Gate and the Upper (Supérieure) Gate; to the north, the Meadow Gate; to the east, Saint Michael's Gate and the Boissarie Gate, to the west, the Forest (Forêt) Gate. The busiest entrances are Saint Michael's and Saint Joseph's Gates.

Saint Joseph's Gate leads, via the Forum (the reception and information centre), to the fore-court of the Rosary Basilica. Saint Michael's Gate, with the Breton Calvary Cross in the foreground and the basilicas in the distance, offers visitors a magnificent view of the Esplanade. More than a kilometre long, this is the shrine's main avenue, and the path followed each day by processions of pilgrims. The southern alley runs alongside the underground basilica of Saint Pius X and its northern pathway beside the John Paul II hostel which also houses the services of the Hospitalité, the medical surgery and the Saint-Côme, Saint-Damien, Père Kolbe and Reconciliation chapels.

The Capital of Prayer

Nearly a century and a half after the apparitions, five million pilgrims and visitors each year come to Lourdes to experience the living reality of Our Lady's message and to bow their heads in prayer in the very places where she once appeared. Here, following in the footsteps of Bernadette, they rediscover in poverty (that is, in humility, and sometimes in pain) the true meaning of prayer and penitence. With so powerful and so universal a message, Lourdes has became a religious capital of international standing. The majority of pilgrims to Lourdes come from a handful of European countries: France (30%), Italy (30%), Spain (10%), Britain (5%), Ireland (5%), Germany (5%) and Belgium (5%). The remaining 10% are drawn to Lourdes from all over the world. Since 1990, a number of believers from eastern European countries, notably Poland, Hungary and Slovakia, have come each year to join the faithful in prayer at Massabielle Grotto. Our Lady of Lourdes is venerated throughout the world, sometimes in a most concrete fashion, for some believers have even made replicas of the Grotto in their own countries. Reports of grottoes and local centres of pilgrimage come from all around the world in such numbers that it is hard to estimate just how many there might really be. Such sites can be found in a number of European countries – Italy, Belgium, Switzerland and Greece – and also in Africa and Asia. In Asia, the cult of Our Lady of Lourdes was spread, in particular, by 19th century missionaries. Even today, there are grottoes dedicated to Our Lady of Lourdes in Japan, Korea, Vietnam, Malaysia, and Burma, with, in Japan, for example, three separate grottoes, in Tamamura, Fukuyama and Nagoya.

At the end of this path is the meeting place for day pilgrims , the statue of the Virgin with Crown, which faces the basilicas. It commemorates the coronation of Our Lady of Lourdes which took place on the third of July, 1876.

The esplanade leads to the square of the Rosary Basilica, defined by the seven large archways supporting the access ramps to the Crypt and to the basilica of the Immaculate Conception, also known as the Upper Basilica. The Marian Procession takes places here every evening from April to October, as does the traditional mass for the end of the Rosary pilgrimage in October.

On the south side, ramps house the Pastorale familiale and *Catéchuménat* catholic lodges and the Esplanade chapel, and on the north side the Masses and Lost Property offices. Pilgrims can seek advice and watch a video film presenting the Message of Lourdes at the information Forum which is in several buildings on the right of Saint Joseph's Gate. Also found here: permanent pilgrimage management, the Entraide Saint-Martin for people in distress, and the Centre d'Action Pastorale which houses the bookshop and is also the head office of the Lourdes sanctuaries Magazine.

Further south near the Immaculate Conception Basilica are the Treasure-house Museum and the entrance to the stations of the Cross. The Grotto opening is to be found in the rocky side of the Massabielle, at the foot of the basilicas, on the left bank of the Gave. The fountains are on its left, and candle sticks and baths on its right. Saint-Bernadette's Church faces it on the opposite bank of the Gave.

There are two medicalised centres on the estate: Notre-Dame and Marie-Saint-Frai, accomodating respectively 900 and 400 patients. The domaine spreads out beyond the Saint Pius X Basilica to the Pavilons area, which is situated between the boulevard de la Grotte and the Gave, at the foot of the old castle.

The Treasure-house Museum

The Treasure-house Museum collections are kept in the ex-premises of the Reconciliation Chapel, near the access to the stations of the Cross. The aim is educational and the display shows the objects as part of the history of art and as landmarks of the history of the sanctuaries and the pilgrimages to Lourdes... which are part of the tradition of the great pilgrimages in the history of France. 19th and 20th century religious arts have a large part to play in the display with chalices, ciborii, monstrances, shrines, liturgical garments which include Monsignor Laurence's mitre, and banners. These objects demonstrate the importance of Lourdes as a pilgrimage centre and underline the fact that Our Lady's request inviting priests to "build a chapel for processions to come to" has been granted.

The *Rose d'Or* of Monsignor Laurence

Museographic Itinerary

Besides the Treasury and the Pyrenees Museums, other museums in Lourdes provide visitors with the possibility of discovering the history and customs of the Pyrenees and provide pilgrims with complementary information about the apparitions and the life of Bernadette Soubirous. They thus prolong their spiritual voyage. The **Lourdes Museum** provides a faithful picture of 19th century rural life. Strolling along the streets and into the houses, visitors can watch different craftsmen at work, discovering for themselves all the secrets of the basket-weaver's workshop, the baker's oven, the cobbler's shop, the mill and the sheepfold. The **Petit Lourdes Museum** takes the visitor on a tour of a miniature version of Lourdes as it was in 1858. Built on a scale of 1:20, it is the

fruit of fifteen years devoted work by its railwayman creator. The **Grévin Museum** (Waxwork Museum) is the only museum of its kind in the world to be devoted exclusively to a religious theme. Run by the famous Parisian waxwork museum of the same name, the museum's five floors house a collection of one hundred and twenty-five life-size wax figures. On the ground floor, they illustrate incidents in the life of Bernadette Soubirous, while on the upper floors, the main events of Christ's life are depicted. The Last Supper, based on Leonardo da Vinci's painting, is one of the museum's highlights. In 1993, a reproduction of the glass casket in which Bernadette's body now lies was added to the collection. The **Nativity Museum** presents a series of fourteen tableaux depicting scenes from Jesus' childhood, from the Annunciation to the incident in the Temple. It also

The Nativity Museum: The manger

The Grévin Museum: Jesus enters Jerusalem

The Lourdes Museum: a spinner

boasts a scale model portraying life in Palestine as Jesus would have known it. On the ground floor, a number of dioramas animated by automatons illustrate different aspects of daily life in the Pyrenees at the end of the last century. The visit to the museum ends with two life-size scenes: the Flight into Egypt and the Nativity. **Saint Bernadette's Museum** on the ground floor of the Our Lady's Pavilion tells the story of the apparitions and of the sanctuaries through a large number of documents and photographs. It exhibits several of the saint's personal objects (including her catechism notebook and her prayer books). Also shown is the beautiful Blue Portrait by Du Roure. The **"Gemmail" Museum**, in the town centre, offers visitors the chance to discover some remarkable compositions executed using this technique. Lourdes is one of the few towns in France to possess a centre dedicated to the little-known art of unleaded stained glass.

The Petit Lourdes Museum: a model of Lourdes as it was in 1858

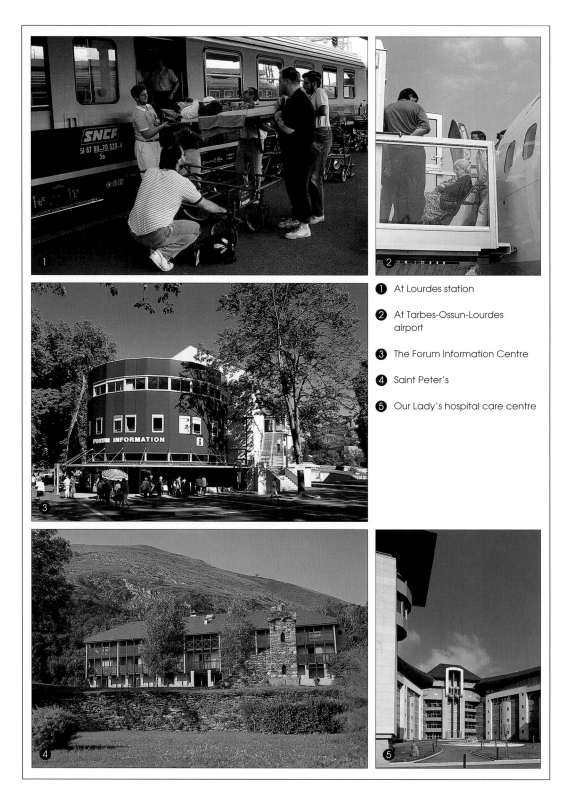

1 At Lourdes station

2 At Tarbes-Ossun-Lourdes airport

3 The Forum Information Centre

4 Saint Peter's

5 Our Lady's hospital care centre

A Welcome For All

The sick and the destitute, the young and the elderly, single people, married couples, entire families; such are the pilgrims to Lourdes. Alone or in groups, they make their way to Lourdes by many different means of transport, but arrive mainly by rail and by air. Each year, Lourdes station receives more than six hundred chartered trains and the nearby airport at Ossun handles nearly five thousand aircraft movements. The shrine welcomes all pilgrims and caters for them according to their individual needs. Maps, programmes of the pilgrimages, and timetables of services and processions are available on request from the reception desk located at each entrance to the shrine, and at the Forum Information Centre on the Esplanade. Visitors can also obtain information and audio and slide presentations from the numerous hostesses, who speak many languages. The sick, travelling with organised pilgrimages, are looked after by voluntary workers, called *hospitallers*, from the moment they arrive at the station or airport. During their stay, they receive free lodging and medical care in one of Lourdes' three hospices. Invalids travelling alone are taken care of by the Lourdes Medical Bureau which, upon presentation of a medical certificate, issues a pass giving priority access to front-row seats during services. The poorest visitors find a welcome at Saint Peter's (the Cité Saint-Pierre), which was inaugurated in 1955 by Monsignor Rodhain, founder of the charity, *Secours Catholique*. Here, poor or abandoned families and individuals, the unemployed and the handicapped are cared for by charitable organisations and the diocesan pilgrimage directorates. Certain foreign visitors have their own special facilities. Sick pilgrims travelling from Britain, for example, can be accommodated and receive medical attention at Hosanna House in Bartrès, while a similar establishment, Across House, caters for British handicapped children.

Thousands of Volunteers Serving the Sick

Lourdes' *hospitallers* can be recognised by their shoulder straps, used, in the past, to carry stretchers. These lay volunteers belong to a network of charities known as *hospitalités*. There are 202 of these worldwide, with 97 in France, all attached to the *Hospitalité* of Our Lady of Lourdes. The diocesan *hospitalités* look after the sick from arrival to departure, meeting them at the station or airport, transporting them to and from the shrine, and caring for them throughout their stay. The hospitallers of Our Lady of Lourdes care for those in hospital and act as stewards in the shrine. Every year, seventy thousand voluntary workers give up their holidays to serve the sick like this. Their "witness to freely given love", as John Paul II put it, is part of the true spirit of Lourdes.

A hospitaller

Lourdes also boasts a medical centre for handicapped children from Ireland and a hospital, the Salus Infirmorum, for the sick from Italy. Since 1984, believers of all nationalities, and in particular those of central European origin (Poles, Hungarians, Czechs, Slovaks, etc.) can be accommodated at the Maison Bellevue. This centre, run by the Polish Catholic Mission, provides spiritual support for the faithful who have come to Lourdes on pilgrimage or retreat.

A chaplain is readily available to say Mass and hear confession every day. Since 1988, a special service for groups has been run by the rectorate. Designed to meet the particular needs of families and independent groups, it provides information and helpful advice for those visitors who, on their own, might find it hard to organise their stay and pilgrimage. During the summer months, one-day pilgrims can be accompanied during their visit by priests, seminarists or specially trained volunteer guides. The one-day programme includes a presentation of the Lourdes message, the Way of the Cross, a celebration of Mass, a guided tour of the shrine or the town, and participation in two of the day's processions. There is no need to book in advance; pilgrims need only turn up at the assembly point at the foot of the statue of the Crowned Virgin at nine in the morning and two-thirty in the afternoon.

The youth camp can accomodate twelve thousand young people and, from July to September, numerous meetings and activities are organised especially for them.

Pilgrims can find an even more personalised response to their individual needs in the shrine's Pavilion area. Run by different Church movements and groups, there are fourteen pavilions in all: the Vocations pavilion, the Handicapped pavilion, the Missionaries pavilion, the Youth Eucharistic Movement pavilion, the Ecumenical Christian Movement pavilion, the Pax Christi pavilion, the Legion of Mary pavilion, and the Families Mission and Catechumenate pavilion.

One-day pilgrims at the foot of the Crowned Virgin

2

"PRAYER AND PENITENCE"

Praying at the Grotto

The silent, private joy of personal prayer that Bernadette experienced during the first apparitions is today shared by the millions of believers who come to pray at the Grotto. The Grotto is the true heart of the Lourdes shrine. The first morning Masses are said there one after the other in every tongue. The ceremony of blessing the children takes place there twice a week. And community prayers for the sick are said there.

The Marian Procession assembles, and at the end of the evening a last mass is performed. Fervent pilgrims continue to touch and embrace the cold, damp sides of the grotto where Our Lady appeared to Bernadette.

The course of the River Gave, which once joined the Savy millstream near the Grotto, has been diverted twice to create a wide forecourt covering an area of twenty-seven square metres. Two paving stones mark the original course of the millstream and the place where Bernadette stood the day of the first apparition. Here, pilgrims bow their heads in silent prayer before the statue of Our Lady, placed on the exact spot where she habitually appeared, in the recess on the right-hand side of the Grotto. At the foot of the statue is a burning bush of candles. Since 1858, following Bernadette's example, the faithful have come to the Grotto bearing candles, the symbol of their faith in Christ, who, in the Gospels, declares, "I am the Light of the world". Inside the Grotto, to the right, a rosebush planted in the rock is a reminder of the "sign" required by the Father Peyramale, who said, "And have her make the rosebush in the grotto blossom". To the left of the altar, visible beneath a pane of glass, is the spring discovered by Bernadette on February 25th, 1858. Harnessed and channelled, its waters are used to supply the nearby drinking fountains and baths.

Millions of Candles Offered Up in Prayer

Every year, more than three million candles are burnt in front of the Grotto. Candles of different sizes are to be found to the left of the drinking fountains. The profits from their sale go mainly towards the upkeep of the shrine. So great is the number of candles bought during the season that it is impossible to burn them all at the same time. Consequently, pilgrims are asked to hold their candles while they are praying, and then to hand them to the staff in charge of the burners (to the right of the Grotto, near the bath-houses). Some of the candles will be kept in a special store and then lit again during the winter months, thus prolonging the pilgrims' prayers well after they have gone.

A candle-burner

The Way of the Cross

Treading the Way of the Cross, pilgrims can re-live in spirit every step along Christ's path to Golgotha. Each pilgrimage to Lourdes organises a collective ceremony, providing the faithful with an opportunity to obey Our Lady's call of "Penitence, penitence, penitence". The Reconciliation Chapel occupies the West of the John Paul II reception centre and encourages the pilgrim to do his first penance: confession. The statue of the priest of Ars, known to say "You should spend more time asking for contrition than in self-examination" is just outside. The first pilgrims had to go to Bétharram to complete their stations of the Cross. A 1200 metre path was traced in 1872 on the Espélugues Hill, also called the Calvary Hill. The 115 two metre high cast iron figures illustrating the various scenes of the Passion were made by the Maison Raffi between 1901 and 1912.The cross at the thirteenth station was brought back from the Holy Land in 1885.

The statue of Jean-Marie Vianney

Jean-Marie Vianney, Curé d'Ars

Born in 1786 to a modest family in Dardilly, Jean-Marie Vianney was very young when he decided to devote his life to religion. In 1815, he was ordained and, in 1817, he was appointed *curé*, or parish priest, to Ars-sur-Formans, a village of two hundred and thirty souls, near Lyons, which had turned away from Christianity during the French Revolution. He remained there until his death in 1859, gradually transforming his parish by his simple and direct preaching, charity and charisma. Even during his lifetime, he had the reputation of a saint. Unlike his contemporaries, who stressed divine justice and obedience to the Law, the *Curé d'Ars* preached a good and merciful God. "God created us and put us on this earth because He loves us," he told his parishioners, "and He wants to save us because He loves us". In 1819, Corpus Christi became a special holiday in the village when he organised the first of what were to become the famous annual processions. In 1824, he founded a free school for the girls of the village, then an orphanage, raising the necessary funds by asking for alms at the roadside. In 1826, his qualities as a confessor began to draw a steady flow of pilgrims to Ars. Known as the "immobile missionary", Jean-Marie Vianney spent his life listening to others and, to the end of his days, devoted himself to the thousands of men and women who came to him in search of forgiveness, hearing confession for twelve to fifteen hours a day. "At the moment of absolution," he would say to these penitents, "God throws our sins over his shoulder; he forgets them, destroying them utterly, so that they will never re-appear." Canonised in 1925, he is now the patron saint of parish priests.

First Station: Jesus is condemned to death. Jesus is shown being brought before Pontius Pilate, Roman governor of Judea. Sentenced to be crucified in the place of Barabbas, he humbly submits to this injustice. The soldiers have plaited him a crown of thorns and dressed him in a purple robe.

Today, this station is missing the statue of Pontius Pilate which was blown up by persons unknown on August 13th, 1983, on the eve of Pope John Paul II's pilgrimage to Lourdes.

Second Station: Jesus takes up his Cross. Holding out his hands to accept the instrument of his death, Jesus chooses to bear the burden of the sins of the world. "No one takes my life from me, but I lay it down of my own accord", he had said the day before.

Third Station: Jesus falls for the first time. Stumbling under the weight of the Cross, Jesus reveals his human nature, in all its weakness.

Fourth Station: Mary joins her son on his way. She shares his suffering, holding out her hands in a gesture of sacrificial giving.

The First Station: "Ecce Homo"

Fifth Station: Simon of Cyrene helps Jesus carry his Cross. The soldiers commandeered Simon as he was coming into the city from the country. Although this condemned man was nothing to Simon, he agreed to carry his Cross. This station challenges us to put Christ's law into practice, as, in the Apostle Paul's words, we "carry each other's burdens".

Sixth Station: Veronica wipes Jesus' face. This woman, moved by the sight of Jesus' face streaked with sweat and blood, comes forward to wipe it, braving the hostility of the crowd.

Seventh Station: Jesus falls for the second time. Leaning heavily on one hand so as not to collapse, he refuses to give in to discouragement.

Eighth Station: The women of Jerusalem weep for Jesus. These women, Jesus' followers, are overcome with grief at seeing so unjust a fate meted out to this innocent man. "Daughters of Jerusalem, do not weep for me," Jesus told them, "Weep for yourselves and for your children."

Ninth Station: Jesus falls for the third time. Completely exhausted, he lies, his face to the ground, while the crowd mocks and sneers.

Tenth Station: Jesus is stripped of his garments. As the Scripture said, "They divided my garments among them, and cast lots for my clothing." The religious leaders have cast Jesus out from their community and handed him over to the Romans who now subject him to that most dreaded form of execution, reserved for criminals: crucifixion.

Eleventh Station: Jesus is nailed to the Cross. As the psalmist foretold, "They have pierced my hands and my feet."

Twelfth Station: Jesus dies on the Cross. "Greater love has no-one than this, that a man lay down his life for his friends." He hangs between two criminals, insulted by the crowd, abandoned by his disciples, except for John, mourned by a few women gathered round Mary, standing at the foot of the Cross. Above his head is an inscription: "The King of the Jews". He forgives his enemies and one of the

thieves, then commends his spirit into his Father's hands. "It is finished", he said, and died.

Thirteenth Station: Jesus' body is taken down from the Cross. At a time when all seems lost, and his followers have fled, Mary is there to take up her son's body.

Fourteenth Station: Jesus is laid in the tomb. Because of the Sabbath, his friends have hurried to wrap his body for burial. They lay him in a new tomb cut into the rock. A heavy stone is placed over the entrance.

Fifteenth Station: The Resurrection. On the third day, after the Sabbath, the women from Galilee make their way to the tomb early in the morning. They have come to embalm Jesus' body. But the stone blocking the entrance has been rolled away and the tomb is empty. A day full of fear, hope and finally joy dawns for Jesus' friends and disciples: He is risen! A second Way of the Cross has been laid out in the Meadow, on the banks of the Gave, as an alternative for the sick and for those who have difficulty getting about.

The Fifteenth Station: The stone of the Resurrection

The Way of the Cross in the Meadow

A Fifteenth Station?

The origins of the devotional exercise of the Way of the Cross go back as far as the 14th and 15th centuries, when the Franciscans began encouraging its observance during Holy Week to commemorate the different episodes of the bearing of the Cross and the Crucifixion. As guardians of the Holy Places of Jerusalem since the 14th century, by virtue of an agreement with the Turkish authorities, they were responsible for directing the devotions of the faithful as they travelled the *Via Dolorosa* in Christ's footsteps. As a sign of penitence, pilgrims were invited to follow the path taken by Jesus from the court of Pontius Pilate in the lower part of Jerusalem, up to Calvary, or Golgotha, "The Place of the Skull". The Franciscans soon had an idea that would allow all Christians to participate in this type of meditation without having to leave the place where they lived: in the open air or inside churches, using pictures, crosses, or statues, they reconstructed the principal stages, known as *stations*, of Christ's sorrowful journey. At each station the faithful were led to meditate. The themes for the stations, which were originally just seven in number, were first established during the 14th century by mystics such as Saint Brigitte. This figure was doubled in the 18th century and approved by Popes Clement XII and Benedict XIV, who gave this meditation on Christ's Passion the form we know today. In 1958, a fifteenth station, evoking the Resurrection, was added to the Way of the Cross at Lourdes. Since then, the practice has become quite widespread and, today, it is not at all unusual to end this spiritually painful journey in prayer before this extra station, "with Mary, in the sure hope of Christ's Resurrection".

3

"GO AND DRINK AT THE SPRING AND WASH IN IT"

The Waters of Massabielle

In the liturgy, and especially in baptism, water is used to symbolise the washing away of original sin. The water from Massabielle Spring, which, according to analysis, is just ordinary drinking water with no real therapeutic properties, was used by Mary – she who was conceived without sin – as, above all, a symbol. To drink it and to wash in it is to rediscover the meaning and grace of that first sacrament, which makes the one baptised "a child of the Church". Imitating Bernadette's gestures, pilgrims find purification of body and soul. A number of craftsmen from Lourdes volunteered to fit out the Grotto, in order to make the spring easily accessible to all. To begin with, a zinc basin equipped with three taps was installed by Castérot, the tinsmith. Nowadays there are thirty-four drinking fountains – actually simple taps – located to the left of the Grotto, where pilgrims can drink and wash their faces in the waters of Massabielle Spring according to the wishes of Our Lady.

Originally, it was the sick who asked to be immersed in the spring water. Accordingly, in 1862, the first wooden bath-house was built. This was replaced, in 1891, by a stone building, before the baths were moved, in 1954, to the right-hand side of the Grotto. The present building houses seventeen stone baths in which the sick and the well alike are immersed by nurses or hospitallers. In this way, nearly four hundred thousand pilgrims a year bathe in the waters of Massabielle Spring.

The baths

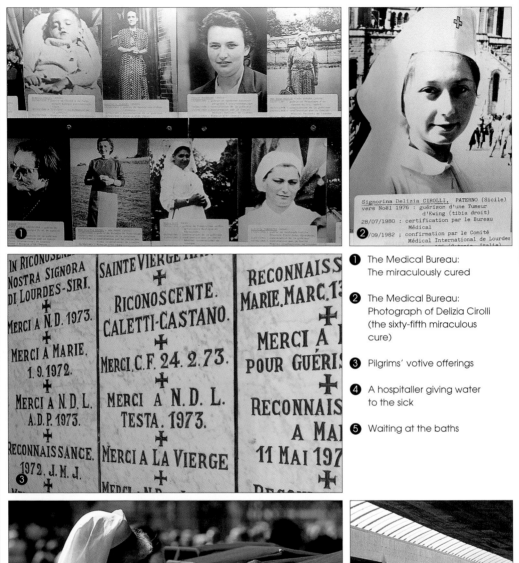

Signorina Delizia CIROLLI, PATERNO (Sicile)
vers Noël 1976 : guérison d'une Tumeur
d'Ewing (tibia droit)
28/07/1980 : certification par le Bureau
Médical
/09/1982 ; confirmation par le Comité
Médical International de Lourdes

IN RICONOSCEN
NOSTRA SIGNORA
DI LOURDES-SIRI.
MERCI A N.D. 1973.
MERCI A MARIE.
1.9.1972.
MERCI A N.D.L.
A.D.P. 1973.
RECONNAISSANCE.
1972. J.M.J.

SAINTE VIERGE
RICONOSCENTE.
CALETTI-CASTANO.
MERCI.C.F. 24.2.73.
MERCI A N.D.L.
TESTA. 1973.
MERCI A LA VIERGE
MERCI N.D.L.

RECONNAISS
MARIE.MARC.13
MERCI A
POUR GUÉRIS
RECONNAIS
A MA
11 MAI 197

① The Medical Bureau:
The miraculously cured

② The Medical Bureau:
Photograph of Delizia Cirolli
(the sixty-fifth miraculous
cure)

③ Pilgrims' votive offerings

④ A hospitaller giving water
to the sick

⑤ Waiting at the baths

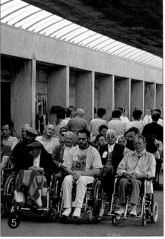

Cures and Miracles

Since the first miraculous cure, of Catherine Latapie, on March 1st, 1858, some 6 784 unexplained healings have been recorded. Of these, however, only 66 have been officially recognised as miraculous by the Church authorities. Each of these cases was the subject of a painstaking inquiry which lasted, in some cases, more than ten years. This lengthy and rigorous procedure has four stages. First, the patient's file is examined by the Lourdes Medical Bureau. Founded in 1883, and known until 1947 as the Bureau of Medical Observations, the Medical Bureau comprises doctors of every nationality, ideology and belief. Its mission is to establish whether the patient had indeed suffered from an organic affliction, attested by several different irrefutable medical examinations, before coming to Lourdes. It must observe that the patient now shows no signs of that illness, that the cure was instant, complete and of a lasting nature, and that it occurred without any treatment or medication being prescribed. The cases that pass these tests move on to the second stage of the procedure, and into the hands of a higher authority, the International Medical Committee. This committee, which was founded as a national organisation in 1947, and became international in 1954, consists of some thirty specialists, and meets each year to re-examine the cases submitted to it. If a cure cannot be explained in medical terms, the case moves on to the third stage and is forwarded to the bishop of the diocese of the person cured. As the fourth and final stage, the canonical commission is consulted. It alone may decide if the cure is a *sign from God*, a miracle, or, in the words of René Laurentin, "the corporal and limited proof of the unlimited grace offered to all". But nowadays, most of the sick who travel to Lourdes come to accomplish a simple act of faith, finding in their pilgrimage moral strength, hope and brotherhood.

The Lourdes Medical Bureau

The examination of the authenticity of any cures that occur in Lourdes remains one of the prime functions of the Lourdes Medical Bureau. Some thirty or so declarations, on average, are transmitted each year to the doctor in charge although, of these, probably no more than two will merit closer examination. Today, the Medical Bureau is beginning to expand its activities, with, for example, the creation of a new information service for the general public. As in the past, pilgrims can still visit the offices of the Medical Bureau to see the photographs and certificates of some of the patients cured. In recent years, they have also been able to attend lectures and discussions on the topic of miracles, held three times a week during the season. The Bureau remains the reception centre for the two thousand volunteer doctors (of the seven thousand registered) who accompany the sick each year. Bound by professional confidence, they may, with the agreement of the doctor in charge, consult the files of cures that are kept at the Medical Bureau secretariat. For the sick travelling to Lourdes independently of the organised pilgrimages, the Medical Bureau also provides a guarantee of security. Of the pilgrims that come to Lourdes, five or six thousand each year receive a patient's card, delivered by the Medical Bureau on presentation of a medical certificate. This card allows them to enjoy preferential treatment throughout the shrine, and, in particular, to be seated during services. The Medical Bureau is also responsible for the upkeep of the shrine's three hospital centres. Finally, it runs two charities comprising members of the medical profession who volunteer to provide free treatment in Lourdes.

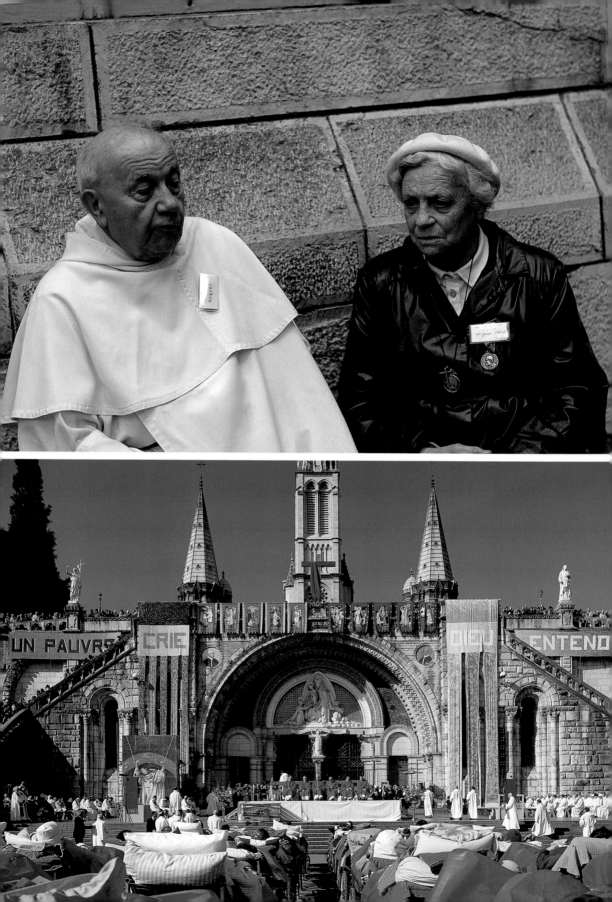

Jeanne Fretel and Lourdes' 52nd Miraculous Cure

Suffering from tuberculous peritonitis, Jeanne Fretel was suddenly cured after taking Holy Communion at Lourdes on October 8th, 1948. Given official church recognition on November 20th, 1950, this cure is one of the unexplained healings known as the "Eucharistic miracles". Together with Father Roques, who gave her Communion, Jeanne Fretel tells her story:

FATHER ROQUES: It was on October 8th, 1948, during the Mass for the sick that was said before the Saint Bernadette altar at half past seven in the morning. When it was time for the Communion, I stepped forward with a ciborium, like the other chaplains. A hospitaller said, "Take this row". I came before a patient lying on her stretcher. There was black blood running from her nose and mouth. Two or three times, I said to her, "Mademoiselle, do you wish to take Communion?" She did not answer. A hospitaller opened Jeanne's mouth with a spoon, and I put a small piece of the Host on her tongue. I closed Jeanne's mouth myself. And then, I must stress this, instantly, and I mean instantly, for that is what makes a Lourdes cure like those recorded in the Gospels, Jeanne opened her eyes, looked at me and said, "Where am I?". I answered, "Mademoiselle, you are in Lourdes", for Jeanne had been in a coma throughout the months of July, August, September and October. She had not eaten properly for six years and could not even keep water down. When she left Rennes, the dean of the faculty, Professor Leplé, who was treating her, had said, "Put a coffin in the luggage van; Jeanne won't make it past Nantes."

JEANNE FRETEL: I don't remember the Communion at all, of course. All I remember is the Grotto where I was lying on a stretcher, and when I got there, it was as though someone was taking me by my hands... by my arms to sit me up. I turned around to look. I couldn't see anyone.

I turned back towards the Grotto and I had that same feeling again, of two invisible hands placed on my stomach.

In those days, when there were two stages in a cure, it was always the first one that counted, which is why my cure has always been considered as a Eucharistic miracle. If the Eucharist had been no more than a symbol, do you really think I'd have been cured?

FATHER ROQUES: When Jeanne realised that the swelling in her stomach had gone down, she went back to Saint Frai's Hospital. To the amazement of everyone, including the doctor, she sat up in bed. "How do you feel?" the doctor asked. "Not bad", she replied, then started to yell, "I'm hungry!" So, they brought her lunch. She had three helpings! Then they did their best to dress her, since she'd come to Lourdes with only her nightclothes. After going to the baths to bathe, she took her medical notes to the Medical Bureau. At the time, Jeanne was being treated in Rennes by Professor Leplé. And I might add, because I am free to say so now, that although he was undeniably an excellent doctor who really cared about his patients, he was a notorious unbeliever. When Jeanne returned to Rennes on the Sunday morning, he said, "Where's Jeanne? Is she dead?"

"Oh, no, Professor, she's here."

"And what's she doing now?"

"Giving injections."

Indeed, Jeanne had gone back to her old work as assistant nurse! He examined her, and at the end of the examination, which lasted quite a while, in front of everyone, he said, "I didn't believe in miracles before, but I do now!" In his lectures at the university, he would say to his students, "That's what happens in Lourdes... Science can't explain it." And when he knew his end was very close, he was quite prepared to ask Jeanne if he could meet a priest to put his conscience in order.

4

"LET A CHAPEL BE BUILT..."

The Crypt

In 1862, Monsignor Laurence, bishop of Tarbes, entrusted the design and the construction of the first chapel to be built at Lourdes to the official *département* architect, Hippolyte Durand. The proposed project consisted of a crypt built into the very heart of Massabielle Rock and a church whose choir was to be located directly above the site of the apparitions. years later, the Crypt was completed and, on May 19th, 1866, it was solemnly inaugurated in the presence of Bernadette. On the pediment above its entrance is a medallion of Pope Pius X, author of the decrees on frequent communion and the communion of children.

The walls of the Crypt and of the long corridors leading to it are covered with ex-voto. The high altar, overlooked by Virgin and Child, an 1868 work of art sculptured by Joseph Fabisch, is enclosed by four chapels dedicated to the Sacred Heart, Saint Peter, Saint Joseph and Saint John the Evangelist. The shrine is in Saint Joseph's chapel and was built by goldsmiths from Lyon -Armand-Calliat-Catelant. Bernadette's fifth right rib , appropriated during the third exhumation in 1925, is housed here. In Winter, the faithful come to the crypt to adore the Blessed Sacrament. This is also possible all through the year at the Adoration Chapel next to Saint Bernadette's church and in Summer, at the Adoration Tent erected in the meadow during the day.

The Crypt

Basilica of the Immaculate Conception

Built directly above the Crypt, its crowned spire rising seventy metres above ground level, the Basilica of the Immaculate Conception, also known as the Upper Basilica, was not opened to the public until 1871. In 1854, Pope Pius IX, author of the dogma of the Immaculate Conception, raised it to the rank of minor basilica. For that reason, the tympanum above the main portal bears his image.

The basilica consists of a single nave, lit by nineteen tall stained-glass windows illustrating the story of the Immaculate Conception from the Earthly Paradise to the proclamation of the dogma in 1854. The nave opens out onto ten chapels dedicated to saints who had a particular veneration for the Virgin Mary.

Two of these chapels, the Chapel of Saint Germaine (the first chapel, to the left of the entrance) and the Chapel of Saint Bertrand of Comminges (the tenth chapel, to the right of entrance) are worth a closer look. The first contains three large marble slabs on which the dates of the eighteen apparitions and the words spoken by the Virgin Mary have been engraved. In the second, pilgrims can read the verdict of Monsignor Laurence's inquiry, proclaiming the apparitions to be genuine.

The stained-glass windows in these chapels tell the story of the Our Lady's apparitions to Bernadette and of pilgrimage to Lourdes. Under the guidance of Canon Lambert of Paris, they were designed and made by Laurent Gsell. To the right of the entrance to the choir, stands a tall statue of the Crowned Virgin. Sculpted by Emilien Cabuchet, it was placed in the basilica in 1876 during the ceremony of the coronation of Our Lady of Lourdes. Around the chevet (behind and on either side of the high altar) there are five more chapels, dedicated respectively to Our Lady of the Rosary, Our Lady of La Salette, Our Lady of Victories, Our Lady of Mount Carmel and Our Lady of Pontmain.

The Upper Basilica: Pius IX's medallion over the portal

The Upper Basilica: The nave

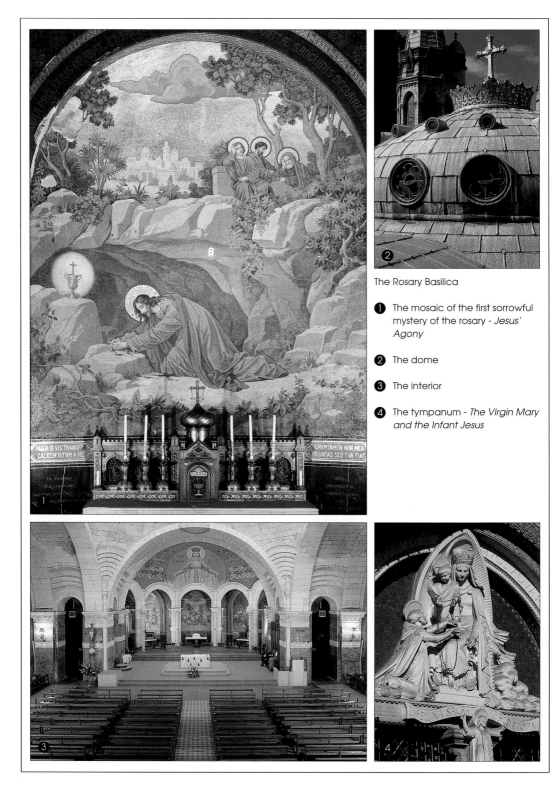

The Rosary Basilica

1 The mosaic of the first sorrowful mystery of the rosary - *Jesus' Agony*

2 The dome

3 The interior

4 The tympanum - *The Virgin Mary and the Infant Jesus*

Rosary Basilica

In 1875, it was decided, with the approval of Pope Pius IX, to build a new church dedicated to the Rosary. Designed and built by the architect Leopold Hardy, it took six years to complete. During construction, the rocky hillside had to be excavated and concrete foundations sunk to a depth of three metres below the level of the River Gave. The church was inaugurated in 1889, consecrated in 1901, and raised to the rank of basilica by Pope Pius XI in 1926. Its dome bears a crown and a cross, commemorating the ceremony of the coronation of Our Lady of Lourdes.

The tympanum above its portal, sculpted by Maniglier, shows Mary and the Infant Jesus giving the rosary to Saint Dominic, who made this form of devotion popular. To the left is a medallion of Pope Leo XIII, who instituted the liturgical festival of the Immaculate Conception, and, to the right, one of Pope Pius XII, who proclaimed the Marian Year of 1954. The Rosary Basilica is neo-Byzantine in style with three naves laid out in the shape of a Greek cross. As soon as they enter the basilica, the faithful are welcomed by the open arms of Our Lady of Lourdes, painted on the vaulted ceiling of the choir by Edgar Maxence in 1920. Many of the pilgrims who visit the basilica recite the rosary, guided by the mosaics in the fifteen side chapels, each of which illustrates one of the Mysteries of the Rosary. The mosaics were produced by Facchina in Paris from 1895 to 1907. The last chapel is of particular interest because the scene of the coronation of the Virgin Mary shows some of the figures who marked the shrine's history in the years 1858 to 1908, the fiftieth anniversary of the apparitions. They include Popes Pius IX, Leo XIII and Saint Pius X, Monsignor Laurence, bishop of the apparitions, Father Sempé, first superior of the Lourdes chaplains, and the miraculously cured Louis Bouriette and Justin Bouhort.

The Mysteries of the Rosary

The word "rosary" comes from a medieval custom of crowning statues of the Virgin Mary with roses. The roses symbolised prayers addressed to Mary. From that custom came the idea of using a string of beads, or chaplet, to guide the prayers. In the 12th century, the Cistercian monks devised a new meditation to go with the beads, and called it the rosary, because they compared it to a mystical crown of roses offered to the Virgin Mary. This devotional exercise was made popular by Saint Dominic in the 13th century. Despite its complicated appearance, it is actually a simple, repetitive prayer, the equivalent of three complete turns around the chaplet. Each decade is accompanied by a mediation or *mystery*, which corresponds to an event from the lives of Mary or Jesus. The first chaplet comprises the five joyous mysteries: the Annunciation, the Visitation, the Nativity, the Presentation in the Temple, and the Conversation with the Teachers of the Law. The second corresponds to the five sorrowful mysteries: the Agony in the Garden of Gethsemane, the Flagellation, the Crown of Thorns, the Bearing of the Cross, and the Crucifixion. The third consists of the five glorious mysteries: the Resurrection, the Ascension, Pentecost, the Assumption, and the Coronation of the Virgin Mary. In some countries, they have maintained the habit of concluding the first part of the *Hail Mary* with a clausula, a short phrase that describes, for each decade, the event to be meditated upon. For example, for the Annunciation, "Jesus is the fruit of your womb" is replaced by "Jesus, whose coming the angel announces to you". These phrases, which may vary, help stimulate concentration and break the repetitiveness of the recitation.

Saint Pius X Basilica

In 1956, in order to accommodate the ever increasing numbers of pilgrims, a huge underground basilica, nearly the size of Saint Peter's in Rome, was built. Dedicated to Pope Pius X, it was consecrated by Cardinal Roncalli (the future Pope John XXIII) on March 25th, 1958, to mark the centenary of the apparitions. The sobriety of this subterranean church contrasts noticeably with the styles of the other buildings of the shrine. Its concrete structure, designed by the architect Pierre Vago, is supported by fifty-eight triangular posts forming twenty-nine porticoes. This design provides maximum visibility and makes best use of the space available. Covering a surface area of some twelve thousand square metres, the basilica is one of the largest buildings in the world, and can hold nearly twenty-five thousand people. Its oval shape has been likened to that of a fish or a grain of wheat, traditional symbols of the Christian Church and of Life. International mass is celebrated here on Wednesday and Sunday mornings. The closing ceremony of the Eucharistic procession and the blessing of the sick also takes place here every afternoon.

The basilica's huge oval hall is entered, from the east and west, by wide access ramps. In the centre, the high altar stands between a fifty-three-stop organ to the south, and, to the north, the papal throne and the seats of the concelebrant priests. The Holy Sacrament is kept in the Pax Christi Chapel, also known as the Chapel of the Holy Sacrament, located behind the high altar in the northern wall of the ambulatory. The altar in this chapel contains a relic of Pope Saint Pius X.

At the far end of the basilica, on the east side, is a third altar, where smaller congregations can gather to hear Mass.

In the centre of this wall, there is a second chapel, dedicated to Saint Theresa of the Christ Child.

Three series of unleaded stained-glass windows, all masterpieces of colour, light the basilica, which has no other decoration. The windows are based on original designs by three prize-winners of the Lourdes International Biennial Festival of Sacred Stained-Glass Art. Set along the eastern ramp are the fifteen stations of the *Path of Burning Love*, an interpretation of the Way of the Cross by Denys de Solère, and along the western ramp, the fifteen *Mysteries of the Rosary* by Robert Falcúcci. Completed in 1993, the third series, *Bernadette's Way of Light*, is based on sketches by René Margotton. Set around the chevet, it depicts the eighteen apparitions and scenes from the saint's life. The basilica also boasts three other remarkable stained-glass compositions: *Bernadette's Vision*, by Marguerite Bordet, *Mary of Light*, by Tony Agostini and *Peter's Boat*, by Meb, which was donated in 1971 to mark the first Faith and Light Pilgrimage for the mentally handicapped. All the windows were crafted by J.-P. and G. Sala-Malherbe.

The Saint Pius X Basilica

The Capital of Sacred Stained-Glass Art

In 1939, the painter Jean Crotti and the physicist Emmanuel Malherbe developed a process that combined glass, colour and light in a new and unique art form that no longer depended on the fragile process of leading. First, the outline of the composition is traced onto a large pane of backlit glass. Next, pieces of multicoloured glass that have been cut, spun or sometimes even moulded, are arranged over the design. Variations in depth of colour are achieved using different thicknesses of glass, and a light adhesive is used to hold the pieces in place during these preparative stages. Finally, the completed composition is put in an oven where the temporary adhesive melts and evaporates in the heat. The

The Saint Pius X Basilica:
The first apparition

The Saint Pius X Basilica:
The second apparition

work of the two inventors was further developed by members of the Malherbe-Navarre family and their pupils. Since 1957, when the Prix du Gemmail (Unleaded Stained Glass Competition) was instituted, under the auspices of Jean Cocteau and Madame Toulouse-Lautrec, this art form has gained international recognition and has been used by many masters of contemporary art. After opening their first museum in

Tours in 1963, and in accordance with the wishes of two young artists, killed in an accident, the gemmistes of France undertook to "bring beauty to Lourdes". Accordingly, Mary's City became, with its International Biennial Festival, the worldwide capital of sacred stained-glass art. Ever since its creation, this art form has held a peculiar fascination for many. In 1993, Cardinal Poupard, president of the Papal Council of Culture, described it in these terms: "Bearer of Beauty, full of Light, a radiant brightness whose depths draw one towards the mysterious presence at its source".

The Saint Pius X Basilica:
The third apparition

The Saint Pius X Basilica:
The seventeenth
apparition

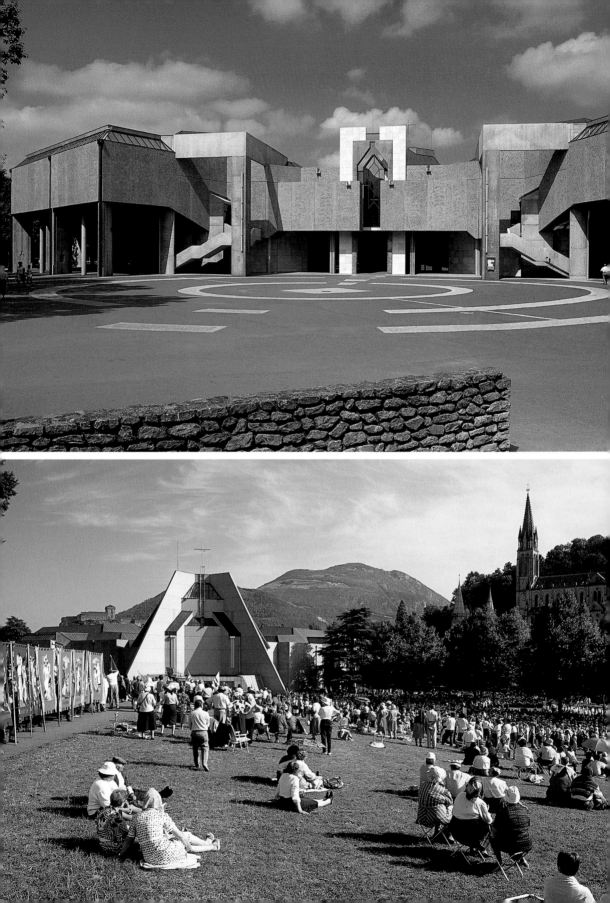

Saint Bernadette's Church

On the left bank of the river stands Saint Bernadette's church, the fourth chapel, dedicated to the saint on the 25th March 1988. This is where Our Lady appeared to Bernadette for the last time. On its West side this church has been flanked by the Adoration Chapel since 1995.

The church is built in the shape of a semicircular amphitheatre which can hold up to five thousand people. It was designed with the specific intention of creating a friendly atmosphere. Mobile partitions can be used to divide the church into two, and eight adjacent rooms can be used for smaller gatherings. To the right of the church is the Mount Carmel lecture-theatre, which seats five hundred. Most of the conferences held during the pilgrimages meet here, and the Annual Conference of the Bishops of France is held here in the autumn.

The vast area around the church, known as the Meadow, is used for open-air masses and special events. This is where, in fine weather, the pilgrimages and the Eucharistic Congresses begin and end. For the Assumption, the Mass, attended each year by eighty thousand pilgrims from all over the world, is traditionally celebrated here. On August 15th, 1983, Pope John Paul II himself said Mass here before a crowd of three hundred thousand believers.

Nearby, an awning, the Velum, covers the podium close to which those who participate in the Eucharistic Procession assemble. A way of the cross for the sick and partly disabled has been traced out on this terrain.

The stations are engraved in the lava along the left bank of the Gave near two circular meeting places where young people prepare the activities for Saturday's mass. Close by is the Adoration Tent where the Holy Sacrament is presented during the Summer.

The interior of Saint Bernadette's Church

5

"LET THE PEOPLE COME IN PROCESSION"

The Eucharistic Procession and the Blessing of the Sick

It was the ceremony organised for the inauguration of the statue of the Virgin Mary in the Grotto, on April 4th, 1864, that was the first to take the form of a true procession, in the liturgical sense, so satisfying, for the first time, Our Lady's request to Bernadette. Led by the local bishop, more than ten thousand people took part. Singing and praying, they assembled at the parish church before making their way through the streets of Lourdes to the Grotto. The blessing of the statue ended with the invocation that was to become traditional, "Our Lady of Lourdes, pray for us". This first pilgrimage was soon followed by many more,

first from neighbouring villages: Loubajac on July 25th, Poueyferré on September 27th, then Bartrès, and so on. Since then, this movement has grown in an unparalleled fashion.

At first, all the processions were *arrival* processions: the faithful assembled at the parish church, and the procession made its way through Lourdes to arrive at the Grotto. But just as the growing numbers of pilgrims began to make progress through the town increasingly difficult, the gradual development of the shrine soon provided plenty of space for them to process unhindered.

After the inauguration of the Crypt, and especially after that of the Basilica of the Immaculate Conception, other habits began to evolve. There seemed to be a natural link between the Grotto and the place where the Holy Sacra-

The Eucharistic Procession

ment was kept; soon, the consecrated Host was brought from the Crypt to the Grotto for the blessing of the sick.

At the Eucharistic Congress on June 25th, 1886, the procession of the Holy Sacrament, comprising ninety thousand believers, followed the newly laid paths of the Esplanade for the first time.

On August 22nd, 1888, during the French National Pilgrimage, the Holy Sacrament was followed from the Basilica to the Grotto by a large number of believers carrying candles. It was during this procession, while the faithful called fervently upon the name of the Christ of the Host, that the first miraculous Eucharistic healing took place: Nina Kin, who had lost the use of her right leg when burnt by sulphuric acid, was instantly cured. The Eucharistic Procession soon became an institution, open to all pilgrims every afternoon.

At present, every afternoon from April to October, the Eucharistic Procession assembles in the meadow surounding the Velum where the Holy Sacrament has just been exposed. The latter, carried on a canopy by an officiating priest, marks the end of the procession. Each diocese and each group walks behind its banner accompanied by its priests, nuns and all its willing sick. Children, young people, adults and the elderly from every country and social background take part in the Eucharistic procession, which portrays in this way a concrete picture of universal brotherhood and the symbol of the faithful moving forward, its members united by the love that is represented by the Eucharist. After crossing the Gave and proceeding before the foot of the Crowned Virgin, they arrive at the basilica of Saint Pius X and assemble around the Holy Sacrament now placed on the altar. Now it is time for adoration and the blessing of the sick. The sick and the healthy both pray for each other. The echo in the large and imposing nave adds to the impressive celebration which ends with a eucharistic hymn and the blessing of the congregation.

The Eucharistic Procession crosses the Gave

The Marian Procession

As early as February 23rd, 1858, on the day of the seventh apparition, Bernadette went to the grotto carrying a candle. She was soon to be copied by many of the faithful. At nightfall on May 11th and 12th, 1858, processions formed near Massabielle Rock. In a report to the *Prefect* (the head of the local civil authorities), Police Superintendent Jacomet described them in the following terms: "Starting out from the grotto, crowds of visitors, many carrying lighted candles, made their way in procession to the entrance to the town, singing liturgical prayers to the Virgin Mary." Soon, these processions became a tradition. Even now, every evening, pilgrims gather before the Grotto. The rosary is recited and then the procession begins its march behind a statue of the Virgin Mary carried by pilgrims. Their light shining in the night creates a powerful image, recalling how, that first Easter morning, the risen Christ "delivered us from the powers of darkness". Seeing this light, the pilgrim cannot fail to remember Christ's own words, when he said, "I am the light of the world. Whoever follows me will never walk in darkness, but will have the light of life."

The long, bright, curving procession is an impressive sight and is the picture of a once individual and henceforward collective testimony. The faithful sing the *Lourdes Ave Maria*, the words of which express the good word announced by the archangel to the Holy Mother. The hymn was composed in 1873 by abbot Gaignet, based on an old Pyrenean tune. Its verses were modified in 1976 by Canon Le Bas and tell the story of the apparitions. The pilgrims, who have been marching side by side, experience a warm feeling of brothership when they gather on the Rosary esplanade to receive the blessing that closes the ceremony. Here they sing their last hommage to the Blessed Virgin, the *Salve Regina*. Brotherly gestures are exchanged before separating and disappearing into the dark Lourdes night. Some will meet again at the Grotto at around 11p.m. where a last mass will be celebrated.

The Marian Procession

The Major Pilgrimages

Today, Lourdes welcomes more than six hundred pilgrimages every year. Its title of *centre mondial de pèlerinage* (worldwide centre of pilgrimage) which, since 1949, has figured on the postmark of every letter and postcard leaving Mary's City, is well-deserved indeed. Almost every country in Europe is represented each year in Lourdes. Five countries organise their own annual national pilgrimages: the Netherlands, Britain, United States, France and Italy.

The oldest of these, the French National Pilgrimage, was founded in 1873 by Assumptionist monks. The young and the sick are the focal point of this pilgrimage, which brings together some twelve thousand people from all over France. In addition, most French dioceses organise their own pilgrimages to Lourdes at different times throughout the year.

The Italian National Pilgrimage, organised by UNITALSI (the Italian National Union for the Transport of the Sick to Lourdes and to the International Shrine), brings nearly ten thousand believers to Lourdes every year. Mobilising nearly as many pilgrims as the French, the Italians are particularly well represented in Lourdes.

Pilgrims are sometimes grouped together according to their professional, social or cultural affinities, for example gypsies, herdsmen or soldiers.

The armed services organise their international pilgrimage each year in May. The first, in 1958, was intended to mark a solemn reconciliation between the nations who had fought each other in the Second World War. Thirty thousand servicemen responded to the call of the pilgrimage organisers. Today, from twenty to twenty-five thousand each year gather together from all over Europe, Africa and Asia, bearing witness to their desire for peace. Finally, associations such as *Secours Catholique* and various Italian Catholic missions,

Youth and Peace

An Italian pilgrimage

and religious communities such as the Redemptorists and the Company of Mary (Monfortain monks), regularly bring their members or followers on pilgrimage to Lourdes.

The largest of these gatherings is, without any doubt, the Pilgrimage of the Rosary. Organised by Dominican monks in the first week of October, forty thousand people each year participate in this event. Preaching and meditation on the mysteries of the rosary occupy a central place. The pilgrimage closes with a High Mass, based on the theme of reconciliation. Traditionally celebrated on the Esplanade, it is one of the highlights of the shrine's liturgical life.

Other large and exceptional gatherings such as Eucharistic congresses and the annual festivities of the 11th February (the anniversary of the first Appearance) and the 8th December (the Immaculate Conception) can be added to the list of pilgrimages. Lastly, the plenary Conference of the Bishops of France meets here each year.

The *Cross of the Sick*

At the Heart of the Pilgrimages: the Sick

"I promise you happiness, not in this world, but in the next." Since 1858, many sick people have seen something of their own lives reflected in the words the Virgin Mary spoke to Bernadette during the third apparition. Each year, some seventy thousand of them come to Lourdes where, led by their faith, they find fellowship and hope. Whether they come as part of a regular diocesan pilgrimage, or with one of the special ones such as the Faith and Light Pilgrimage for the handicapped, Cancer Hope, or the Handicapped Children's Pilgrimage Trust, the sick hold a central place in all the major pilgrimages, especially in the Pilgrimage of the Rosary and the French National Pilgrimage.

During each of these pilgrimages, a special service, known as the *Anointing of the Sick*, is organised. The ceremony often takes place during Mass. On the last day of the Pilgrimage of the Rosary, the sick and the well alike come together for this celebration, which becomes a particularly solemn occasion. Facing the altar, on the forecourt of the Rosary Basilica, the sick are laid out on their stretchers in the highly symbolic form of a cross. First, the congregation asks God for forgiveness. Then, the priest anoints with holy oil the forehead and hands of the men and women who are presented to him. This sacrament recognises and sanctifies the trials and tribulations experienced daily by these people. In this way, the Church commends the sick to the Lord, and calls upon them to accept the cross they each have to bear. This sacrament is offered to those whose health is beginning to be seriously affected by illness or age, and those about to undergo an operation.

John Paul II, Pilgrim

Shortly before his departure at the end of his pilgrimage to Lourdes on August 15, 1983, Pope John Paul II admitted, "It is not without regret, it is not without nostalgia that a pilgrim must leave a place so full of grace. All the more Peter's successor who, like Bernadette, was able to approach the place where the Immaculate Conception showed her face and said her name, was able to lay down the heavy intentions of her universal burden and pray with a people of believers." Twenty-one years later, on August 14th and 15th, 2004, on the occasion of the one hundred and fiftieth anniversary of the promulgation of the dogma of Immaculate Conception, the Holy Father returned to Lourdes, responding to the invitation of Monseigneur Jacques Perrier, Bishop of

John Paul II at the Grotto on August 15, 2004, before leaving for Rome

John Paul II during mass on August 15, 2004

Tarbes and Lourdes. On August 14th, John Paul II addressed the sick in front of the Massabielle grotto, "the end of his pilgrimage". "Dear ill brothers and sisters, I would like to hold you in my arms, one after the other, in an affectionate way, and tell you how close I feel to you and am standing by you." And on August 15th, before an enormous, enthusiastic and attentive crowd, gathered in a field in radiant sunshine, he pronounced his homily. Under the circumstances, he returned to the dogma of Immaculate Conception. "Today the Church celebrates Mary's glorious Assumption body and soul into Heaven.The two dogmas of the Immaculate Conception and the Assumption are closely related. Both proclaim the glory of Christ the Redeemer and the holiness of Mary, whose human destiny is even now perfectly and definitely realized in

John Paul II among the faithful in the afternoon of August 14, 2004

God." The Pope then addressed the young people who would find in Lourdes "an answer capable of giving meaning to (their) lives", "a demanding answer (which) contains the secret of true joy and peace." To women, "to whom falls the task of being sentinels of the Invisible", the Pope said, "I appeal urgently to all of you to do everything in your power to ensure that life, each and every life, will be respected from conception till its natural end." The Holy Father insisted that "life is a sacred gift and nobody can presume to be its master". And the sovereign pontiff concluded by saying, "Our Lady of Lourdes has a message for everyone. Be men and women of freedom! But remember: human freedom is a freedom wounded by sin. It is a freedom which itself needs to be set free. Christ is its liberator". Before leaving Lourdes in the evening of that memorable August 15th, John Paul II worshipped deeply and at length before the rock of Massabielle, bathed in the beautiful light of the end of a summer afternoon, in the impressive silence of an equally impressive crowd, ever-present just a few metres away, communicating with the Pope during his prayers.

INDEX